RETIREMENT

CAUSES AND CONSEQUENCES

Erdman B. Palmore, Ph.D., is Professor of Medical Sociology and Senior Fellow at the Duke Center for the Study of Aging and Human Development. He has published several articles on retirement in professional journals and has written or edited nine books in the field of aging. He received his B.A. from Duke University, M.A. from the University of Chicago, and Ph.D. from Columbia University. He is currently President of the Southern Gerontological Society, and is working on two research projects: "Mental Illness and Social Support among the Very Old" and "The Effects of Institutionalization on the Aged."

Bruce M. Burchett, Ph.D., is a senior data technician at the Duke Center for the Study of Aging and Human Development. He received his B.A. from the University of North Carolina and his M.A. from Carlton University, Ottawa, Canada. He recently completed his doctoral dissertation on the administration of military justice in the United States Army.

Gerda G. Fillenbaum, Ph.D., is a Research Associate in the Department of Psychiatry and Senior Fellow at the Duke Center for the Study of Aging and Human Development. She has published several articles on retirement in professional journals, as well as research on functional assessment of the elderly. A monograph on functional assessment is currently in press. Her research also includes the living arrangements of the elderly. Her undergraduate and graduate degrees were from the University of London and she did postdoctoral work in aging at the Center for the Study of Aging and Human Development.

Linda K. George, Ph.D., is Associate Professor of Medical Sociology and Senior Fellow at the Duke Center for the Study of Aging and Human Development. She is the author of three books and numerous chapters and journal articles in the area of aging. Several of her previous publications have addressed issues of work and retirement. Dr. George received her B.A. and M.A. from Miami University and her Ph.D. at Duke University. She currently is Social Sciences Editor for the *Journal of Gerontology* and holds elected offices in both the Gerontological Society of America and the Southern Gerontological Society. Dr. George's current research projects include studies of stress and coping, caregiver burden among family members caring for impaired older adults, and the epidemiology of psychiatric disorders during later life.

Laurence M. Wallman is a Research Associate at the Center for the Study of Aging and Human Development and a statistical consultant in the Center's Computing and Statistical Laboratory. He received his B.S. from Rensselaer Polytechnic Institute and his M.A. from Duke University. He is currently doing graduate work in the Department of Statistics at the University of North Carolina, Chapel Hill, and is a member of the American Statistical Association.

RETIREMENT
CAUSES AND CONSEQUENCES

Erdman B. Palmore, Ph.D.
Bruce M. Burchett, Ph.D.
Gerda G. Fillenbaum, Ph.D.
Linda K. George, Ph.D.
Laurence M. Wallman, M.A.

SPRINGER PUBLISHING COMPANY
NEW YORK

Springer Publishing Company, Inc.
200 Park Avenue South
New York, New York 10003

85 86 87 88 89 / 10 9 8 7 6 5 4 3 2 1

Library of Congress Cataloging in Publication Data

Main entry under title:
Retirement: causes and consequences
   Bibliography: p. Includes index.
   1. Retirement—United States. I. Palmore, Erdman Ballagh
HQ1064.U5R398 1985   306'.38   84-16057
ISBN O-8261-4720-8

Printed in the United States of America

*To the thousands of respondents
who made this book possible.*

Contents

Contents

Preface

This book reports the results of the most comprehensive and definitive study of the causes and consequences of retirement ever undertaken. The grounds for this statement are discussed in Chapter 1. This study grew out of the commitment of the Duke Center for the Study of Aging and Human Development for "research in service to the aging." We believe this research will be of such service (see Chapter 11).

The Center began almost 30 years ago (1955) with the First Duke Longitudinal Study of Aging. This study and the Second Duke Longitudinal Study of Aging were both dedicated to learning more about the processes of normal aging, including such processes as retirement (Palmore, 1970; 1974).

The retirement study was also an outgrowth of the Duke Data Archives on Aging and Adult Development which began in 1976. It now contains data from 69 sources. (For information on the Duke Data Archive, contact Dr. Linda George at the Duke Center.) Included in this archive are the seven longitudinal studies of retirement used in our analyses. This facilitated easy access to the several complex data sets.

The retirement study was made possible by a grant from the National Institute on Aging during 1980–83 (#AG-02023), and we are grateful to them for their support—as well as to the taxpayers whose taxes support the National Institute on Aging. Computations for this study were done in the Duke Gerontology and Statistical Laboratory, which is primarily funded by NIA grant AG00371.

Previous versions of Chapters 3 and 4 have been published in the *Journal of Gerontology* (Palmore, Fillenbaum, & George, 1982; 1984). Other versions of various chapters have been presented at several professional meetings and/or submitted for publication to professional journals. This book contains all the findings from these presentations and publications.

All five of the authors contributed to each of the chapters in one way or another. However, primary responsibility for the analysis and writing of the chapters was as follows:

Palmore—Chapters 1, 3, 4, 6, and 11.
Fillenbaum—Chapters 7, 9, and 10.
George—Chapters 5 and 8.
Burchett and Wallman—Chapter 2 and Appendix.

Erdman Palmore was project director, Gerda Fillenbaum and Linda George were co-investigators, Larry Wallman was statistician, and Bruce Burchett was computer programmer. Kay Bailey provided typing and secretarial services.

We believe the topics in these chapters will be of interest to most adults concerned about retirement. While the statistical analysis may be difficult to understand for those not familiar with these methods, we hope the interpretation and meaning of all the analyses will be clear to all readers.

1
Introduction

Almost every adult has (or should have) a personal concern about retirement. Most workers are concerned about whether the combination of their social security benefits, pensions, and savings will produce adequate retirement income. Such concerns are unusually worrisome during these times of high and fluctuating inflation rates. Fears that the social security system may "go bankrupt" add to this concern. Younger workers may be concerned that their social security "contribution" will be more than they get back in benefits. Many workers worry about whether they are saving enough to assure a comfortable retirement. Older workers may wonder when or if they should retire. They may have difficulty deciding whether the joys and benefits of retirement outweigh the loss of income, status, and purpose that retirement may cause. They may fear that retirement causes declines in health, happiness, activities, and even early death. Others are only concerned to retire as early as possible. Persons who have already retired may wonder whether they would be better off returning to work. Such concerns affect not only the retiree, but the retiree's spouse also.

As American citizens we may all be concerned about how retirement rates affect our economy, our taxes, our welfare programs, and the quality of life among our older citizens.

This almost universal concern with retirement is a recent phenomenon. At the turn of the century few were concerned because retirement was not a viable option for most. Most workers worked as long as they were physically and mentally able. Even as late as 1930, more than half of the men over age 65 continued in the labor force.

The development of retirement as a viable option for most older workers was dependent on two prerequisites: an industrial economy productive enough to provide the economic surplus necessary to support retirement of most older workers, and the institutionalization of retirement through adequate public and private pension systems. Part of the institutionalization of retirement has been the growing acceptance of the idea that older workers have a *right* to retire by virtue of many years of service at a job. During the decades since World War II the majority of the public has shifted from justifying retirement only if the individual is physically unable to continue work, to justifying retirement on the basis of prior service (Ash, 1966).

Indeed, despite the passage of laws preventing compulsory retirement before age 70, many people still believe that older workers have a *duty* to retire in order to "make room for younger workers" (Harris, 1981).

CONCEPTS AND DEFINITIONS

Because of this widespread concern with retirement, many people use the term in many different ways. Retirement has been thought of as an event, a process, a role, or a phase of life (Atchley, 1976). Each of these conceptualizations is useful and valid.

Retirement as an event may include the retirement ceremony (dinner or party), the presentation of a retirement present (traditionally a watch), the paper work for receiving retirement pension and social security benefits, the cleaning out of desk or locker, the turning in of keys, and the Retirement Trip (often to foreign countries or even around the world).

Retirement as a process includes preparation for retirement, the decision to retire, the actual retirement event, the "honeymoon phase" (in which the retiree enjoys the novel freedom from work), sometimes the "disenchantment phase" (in which the novelty of retirement wears off and the problems appear), followed by a "reorientation phase" (in which the retiree finds new interests and activities to replace the job), and the "termination phase" (in which the retirement role is ended by return to work, disability, or death) (Atchley, 1976).

Retirement as a role is made up of general social norms regarding the rights and duties of the position called "retired person." It is not a "roleless role," as some have asserted (Burgess, 1960). The rights of a retired person include the right to economic support without holding a job and without the stigma of being unemployed; the right to respect for years of service; the right to autonomy concerning the management of one's time; and often specific rights such as the right to use company or union facilities, to continue health insurance through the company, etc. The duties of retired persons include the duty to assume responsibility for managing their own lives; the duty to live within their retirement income so as to avoid financial dependence on the family or state; and the duty to take care of their health so as to avoid physical dependence on others. In addition to these rights and duties, retired persons continue the rights and duties associated with all their other roles such as family member, church or club member, and citizen.

Retirement as a phase of life usually comes late in the life cycle, usually in the 60's after about 40 years of employment, and usually in the family cycle after the last child has left home (the "child free" stage). Most retired persons enjoy (or endure) about 15 to 20 years of life in this phase.

The present research conceives of retirement primarily as a process with identifiable predictors and multiple consequences. Our primary purpose is to analyze the predictors and consequences of retirement and how they vary by reason for retirement, age at retirement, gender, race, and socioeconomic level. We also analyze predictors of adjustment to retirement and return to work after retirement.

We use three primary definitions of retirement in this analysis:

1. Subjective Retirement. This was based on the respondent's assessment of his/her own retirement status.
2. Objective Retirement. This was based on working less than full-time and receiving a retirement pension.
3. Amount of Employment. This was an interval scale measure of retirement and was based on the number of hours worked in the past year. Those who worked no hours were fully retired; those who worked less than full-time were partially retired; and those who worked full-time were not retired. (See Chapter 2 for more details.)

The reason for using the above three different definitions of retirement in our analysis was that we wanted to examine whether the different definitions produced different results in terms of predictors and consequences of retirement. Certainly the number of persons defined as retired varies with the definition. Palmore (1967) found that only 64 percent of men 65 and over had no work experience in the previous year, but 80 percent received some kind of retirement pension, and 87 percent worked less than full time year-round.

PREVIOUS RESEARCH

Because of the many concerns about retirement, it is one of the most researched topics in gerontology. The research relevant to particular aspects of retirement are reviewed in the appropriate chapters that follow. However, all of the previous research suffers from several of the following weaknesses:

1. Cross-sectional. The weakness of cross-sectional research is that it cannot distinguish causes from effects of retirement. For example, when cross-sectional studies find that retired persons have less income than working persons, they cannot tell whether this is because persons with lower incomes are more likely to retire or because retirement reduces income (our analysis shows that both explanations are partially true).

2. Local Samples. The weakness of research based on samples from one local area is that we cannot tell how representative the findings are of retirement in other areas. We have analyzed data from some local studies for comparison with the findings from nationally representative samples and found marked differences between them. Data from local samples can be useful supplements to the data from the national samples, but only when the national data is used to evaluate the representativeness of the local samples.

3. Bivariate Analyses. Most of the analyses in previous research have analyzed only two or three variables at a time. The weakness of this approach is that it cannot tell whether a given association may be partially due to associations with a third or fourth variable, or may be entirely due to chance, when other variables are controlled. Retirement is a complex phenomenon influenced by and having effects upon multiple variables. Multi-variate statistical techniques are the only way to isolate the unique effects of each variable and to examine the complex interrelationships among them.

4. Lack of Appropriate Comparisons. Some of the longitudinal studies have analyzed changes among retired persons over time; but without comparisons to the changes among comparable per-

sons who continue to work, we cannot tell whether the changes were caused by retirement or not.

5. Single Measures of Retirement. Most of the previous research used only one definition of retirement. As a result we do not know whether similar results would have been found with an alternate definition of retirement.

6. White Males Only. Most of the previous research has been based on samples of white males only. As a result, we do not know whether their findings apply to women and blacks. Furthermore, differences in retirement between upper and lower socioeconomic groups, between those retiring early or later, between those who retire voluntarily or involuntarily, and between those who return to work and those who do not, have received little attention.

To overcome these weaknesses, our analyses:

1. are based on longitudinal studies;
2. are based on several nationally representative samples, supplemented with quality studies representative of local areas;
3. use appropriate multivariate statistical techniques;
4. include appropriate comparison with nonretired persons;
5. use multiple definitions of retirement; and
6. compare differences in retirement between men and women, blacks and whites, upper and lower socioeconomic groups, early and late retirees, voluntary and involuntary retirees, fully retired and returners to work.

CONCEPTUAL MODEL

Figure 1.1 presents a conceptual model for our analyses of the predictors and consequences of retirement. The rectangle on the left shows the major objective and subjective predictors examined. The dotted square below shows that the outcome measures are measured before retirement in order to establish baselines for change in the consequences. The middle rectangle shows our three alternate definitions of retirement. The rectangle on the right shows the major objective and subjective consequences examined. It should be clear that this is a general conceptual model, not an empirically testable one. Specific models for testing are presented

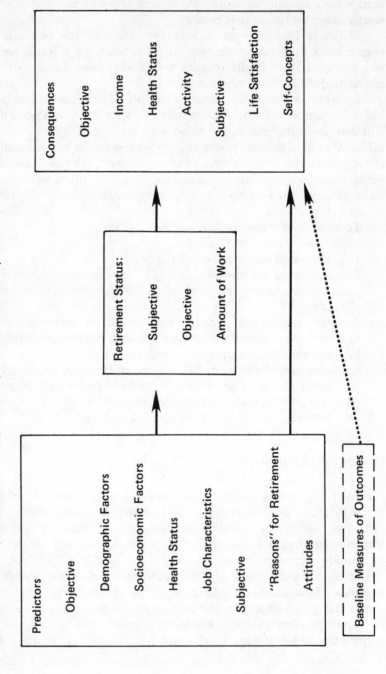

FIGURE 1.1. Conceptual model for analysis of the predictors and consequences of retirement.

Predictors

Objective

Demographic Factors

Socioeconomic Factors

Health Status

Job Characteristics

Subjective

"Reasons" for Retirement

Attitudes

Retirement Status:

Subjective

Objective

Amount of Work

Consequences

Objective

Income

Health Status

Activity

Subjective

Life Satisfaction

Self-Concepts

Baseline Measures of Outcomes

in subsequent chapters. Because this is such a comprehensive model and because our analyses overcome the weaknesses of previous research, we believe this monograph represents the most definitive study of retirement ever undertaken.

ORGANIZATION OF THE BOOK

The next chapter explains the methods used in our analyses: the seven data sets used, the measures of retirement, description of the samples, and the statistical models used for analysis. Chapters 3 and 4 present the predictors and consequences of retirement among men as well as differences between early and later retirees. Chapter 5 analyzes which factors predict better adjustment after retirement. Chapter 6 presents the differences between those who retire voluntarily and those who retire involuntarily. Chapter 7 presents the differences between those who return to work after retirement and those who do not. Chapter 8, 9, and 10 present the differences between men and women, blacks and whites, and between socioeconomic levels. The final chapter summarizes the major findings and discusses their implications for social policy. All the variables found significant in these analyses are described in the Appendix. There is an index at the end for easy reference to topics of previous studies.

2
Methodology

In this chapter we shall discuss two aspects of the research methods: the data bases upon which the research was performed, and the statistical tests utilized in the analyses. In discussing the data base, we shall present some demographic and socioeconomic characteristics of the persons in the samples and discuss the measures of retirement employed.

As the purpose of this research is to study both the predictors and the consequences of retirement, it was necessary that the data sets be multi-wave, that is, that they contain longitudinal data. Seven data sets were selected to comprise the data base of the research. They are:

1. The Retirement History Study (RHS), which was conducted by the Social Security Administration during the years 1969 to 1979. At the time of the analyses, data through 1975 were available. The data were collected every two years; therefore there are four waves in the study: 1969, 1971, 1973, and 1975. RHS started with a nationally representative sample of 11,153 men and unmarried women between the ages of 58 and 63 in 1969. The RHS contains detailed information on demographic and economic variables, work history, health, and limited social-psychological characteristics (Murray, 1979).

2. The National Longitudinal Surveys (NLS) were conducted for the Department of Labor by the Center for Human Resources Research (Ohio State University) during the years 1966 to 1976. The NLS were initially based on a nationally representative sample of 5020 men between the ages of 45 and 59, with blacks being oversampled by three to one. Although data were collected each year, the scope of the data varied considerably from year to year. In our research, we concentrated on data collected in 1966, 1971, and 1976. These three waves contained relatively complete information from those in the sample and served to divide the research

into equidistant time intervals. The NLS contain detailed demographic, economic, and work history information; and limited social psychological information (Parnes, 1981).

3. The Panel Study of Income Dynamics (PSID) was conducted by the Institute for Social Research of the University of Michigan from 1968 to 1977. The PSID started with a nationally representative sample of 5000 families in 1968. Although data were collected yearly, we concentrated on the years 1968, 1971, 1974, and 1977. The PSID contains detailed demographic, economic, and work history information; moderate health information; and limited social psychological information (Morgan & Duncan, 1980).

4. The Duke Work and Retirement Study (DWRS) was conducted by the Center for the Study of Aging and Human Development at Duke University during the years from 1961 to 1966. It started with a sample of 467 men, either retired or within five years of retirement, from the Piedmont area of North Carolina and Virginia. This study provided a two-wave study. DWRS contains detailed demographic and social psychological information; and moderate economic, work history, and health information (Simpson & McKinney, 1966).

5. The Duke Second Longitudinal Study (DSLS) was conducted by the Center for the Study of Aging and Human Development, Duke University, during the period from 1969 to 1976. It started with a representative sample of 502 men, aged 46 to 70, from the Durham, North Carolina, area. The study provided four waves for the analyses. DSLS contains detailed demographic, health, and social psychological data; and moderate economic and work history information (Palmore, 1974).

6. The Ohio Longitudinal Study (OLS) was conducted by the Scripps Foundation during the years 1975 to 1981. The study contains four waves of which the first two were available to the present study. It started with a representative sample of about 1100 men and women, aged 50 to 94, living in a small town located in a metropolitan area in Ohio. OLS contains detailed demographic and social psychological information; and moderate economic, work history, and health information (Atchley, 1982).

7. The Michigan Study of Auto Workers (MSAW) was conducted by the Institute of Social Research, the University of Michigan, during the period from 1966 to 1969. The study provided two waves of data for analysis. MSAW started with a representative sample of 3647 men and women, aged 35 to 59, who were auto workers in Michigan. Its purpose was to study the effects of

a new pension policy on early retirement. The study contains detailed demographic and economic information, but limited health and social psychological data (Barfield & Morgan, 1969).

INCLUSION CRITERIA FOR THE RESEARCH

Some of the subjects examined by the above studies were not suitable for inclusion in our data base. At the onset, we established four conditions which must be satisfied in order for a case to be included in our research. They were: (1) the subject must be present in all waves; (2) the subject must be at least 50 years of age at the onset of the study; (3) the subject must not be retired at the beginning of the study; and (4) the subject must be working at least 16 hours a week at the beginning of the study. These inclusion criteria, in particular point 3, were relaxed in certain studies concerned with postretirement adjustment.

MEASURES OF RETIREMENT

Five major measures of retirement were constructed and employed in the analyses. They were: subjective retirement, objective retirement, time of retirement, age at retirement, and amount of employment. Each of these will be presented and its construction discussed for the several data sets.

1. Subjective Retirement. Subjective retirement was based upon the respondent's assessment of his own retirement status. This was coded as a dichotomous measure.

2. Objective Retirement. Objective retirement was based upon the number of hours worked by the respondent and whether or not he was receiving a pension when that information was available. In RHS a person was said to be objectively retired if he worked less than 35 hours per week and was receiving a retirement pension. In NLS insufficient pension data were available; therefore a person was said to be objectively retired if he worked less than 35 hours a week. In PSID those working less than 1700 hours a year and receiving a pension were said to be objectively retired. In DWRS no pension data were present; a person was said to be objectively retired if he worked less than 35 hours a week. No pension data were present for DSLS; those working less than full-time were classified as being objectively retired. In OLS those working less than full-time and receiving a pension were said to be objectively retired. No measures of work hours were available for the MSAW; therefore no measure of objective retirement was possible. Objective retirement, like subjective retirement, is a dichotomous measure.

3. *Time of Retirement.* Those who retired before age 65 were said to be early retirees. Those who retired at age 65 were said to have retired on time, and those who retired after age 65 were said to be late retirees. In the analyses undertaken, primary interest was in those who retired early. In RHS, NLS, and PSID those who retired according to the objective measure prior to age 65 were classified as early retirees. In DSLS and MSAW questions were asked of the respondents as to their age of retirement. Those who stated that they retired before reaching age 65 were said to be early retirees. Data were not available concerning the age of retirement for DWRS and OLS. Time of retirement was treated either as an ordinal measure (early—on time—late) or constructed into dummy variables (early vs. all others). In most analyses the dummy variable was used.

4. *Age at Retirement.* In NLS and PSID the respondent's age at the wave in which he first met the criteria for objective retirement was taken as the age of retirement. In DSLS and MSAW the age at which the respondent stated he had retired was considered to be the age of retirement. In DWRS, RHS, and OLS insufficient information was available to calculate the age at retirement.

5. *Amount of Employment.* In contrast with the first two measures of retirement, this measure was constructed as an interval scale. This measure was based on the number of hours worked by the respondent. In RHS the amount of employment was determined by taking the number of hours worked by the respondent in the previous two years, in thousands. In NLS and PSID the number of hours employed in the past year was taken as the measure of employment. In DWRS the amount of employment was based on the number of hours employed per week by the respondent. In DSLS the number of months employed in the past year was the measure of amount of employment. In OLS, respondents were classified according to whether they did not work at all, worked part-time, or worked full-time. MSAW did not contain data for this measure.

In addition to the above, measures were constructed to indicate whether the respondent retired for voluntary reasons as opposed to retiring because of having reached a mandatory retirement age, having retired for reasons of health, for job related reasons, or for other involuntary reasons.

DESCRIPTION OF THE SAMPLES

Although the data sets are all longitudinal in nature and several are taken from national samples, there is considerable variation between the data sets with respect to the demographic and socioeconomic characteristics of the samples. Table 2.1 presents selected statistics that describe the various samples.

Age

The minimum age for inclusion in any of the samples was 50 years of age at Time 1. There was, however, no maximum age for inclusion within the general samples. In specific analyses maximum ages were often specified. Some of the data sets did have cutoff ages for the respondents. In addition, two aspects of the selection criteria would tend to affect the maximum age: the respondents analyzed had to be working at Time 1 and present in all waves.

All of the persons in the RHS sample were between 58 and 63 years of age at Time 1. In NLS all of the respondents were between 50 and 59 years of age in the first wave. In MSAW 79 percent were in their 60s at the initial time period with none 65 or over. It is important to bear in mind that the purpose of MSAW was to experiment with a new retirement pension plan. Both PSID and DSLS had respondents in their 70s, though the percentages varied considerably, being 9 percent and 1 percent respectively.

Gender

The sex composition of the data sets also varied considerably. In addition to the selection criteria of the original data sets, the selection criteria used in our analysis could affect the gender distribution of those in our samples. Since women were less likely to be working than were men of the ages studied, this was reflected

TABLE 2.1
Demographic Characteristics of Study Samples
Meeting Selection Criteria
(Percentage Distributions)

	DSLS	DWRS	MSAW	NLS	OLS	PSID	RHS
Sex							
Male	68.9	100.0	100.0	100.0	43.5	69.4	79.6
Female	31.1	0.0	0.0	0.0	56.5	30.6	20.4
Age							
50-54	30.1	0.0	0.0	54.1	19.3	31.0	0
55-59	36.6	4.3	21.1	45.9	20.2	28.0	40.0
60-64	20.2	63.8	78.9	0	17.8	18.7	60.0
65-69	12.0	23.9	0.0	0	14.4	13.0	0
70-74	1.1	7.3	0.0	0	14.0	7.4	0
75+	0.0	0.7	0.0	0	14.3	1.9	0
Race							
White	100.0	100.0	84.4	69.5	95.1	70.9	91.4
Black	0.0	0.0	15.6	28.6	4.8	27.8	8.6
Other	0.0	0.0	0.0	1.9	0.1	1.3	0.0
Education							
<High school	22.4	43.5	45.9	50.8	6.5	16.8	37.8
Some high school	15.8	13.0	31.5	18.5	6.2	15.3	19.1
High school	20.8	5.3	10.0	17.3	17.5	33.6	24.6
Some college	15.8	3.1	11.3	6.3	16.1	16.0	9.0
College graduate	10.4	2.3	1.3	3.8	14.6	10.3	5.4
Graduate school	14.8	32.8	0.0	3.3	39.1	8.0	4.1
Marital Status							
Married	90.7	91.3	88.4	86.4	74.1	60.6	72.2
Widowed	6.1	2.9	3.8	3.2	14.6	24.6 ⎫	
Separated/divorced	1.6	2.9	3.8	5.9	5.3	10.2 ⎬	27.8
Never married	1.6	2.9	4.0	4.5	6.0	4.6 ⎭	
Total Number	183	138	552	3185	851	1120	1845

in the composition of our samples. Three of the data sets, DWRS, MSAW, and NLS, contained only males. RHS did not contain any married women; all of the women in the sample were unmarried working women. Two-thirds of the respondents in PSID and DSLS were men. OLS, on the other hand, was the only data set in which women constituted a majority of the respondents (57%).

Race

There was also considerable variation between the data sets with regard to the race of the respondents. In DSLS and DWRS all of the respondents were white. In PSID and NLS blacks were over-sampled by approximately three to one. In MSAW the white:black ratio was roughly 6:1. In RHS blacks were approximately 9% of the total sample. OLS was 95% whites, reflecting the racial charac-teristics of the Midwestern area in which the study was done.

Marital Status

Except for RHS (see above), the respondent's marital status did not directly affect the selection of those in the sample. Seventy-two percent of those in RHS were married at Time 1. In PSID the percentage of those married was 61%; 10% were separated or di-vorced; 25% were widowed; and 5% had never married. In OLS 74% of the respondents were married, 5% were separated or di-vorced, 15% were widowed, and 6% had never been married.

The remaining data sets displayed somewhat different patterns with respect to marital status. In the MSAW study, 88% of the re-spondents were married; 4% were separated or divorced; 4% were widowed; and 4% had never been married. The major difference in this data set is the lower percent widowed. This is because the sample consisted of male automobile workers, none of whom had reached the mandatory retirement age.

NLS also had a high percentage of married respondents. Eighty-six percent of those in the sample were married, 6% were sepa-rated or divorced, 3% were widowed, and 5% had never married.

Again the percentage widowed is much lower than found in the other samples. In NLS, as in MSAW, the sample consisted exclusively of men. Since women tend to outlive men, there are fewer widowed males than widowed females. In addition, none of those in NLS were older than 59 years of age at Time 1.

The percentage of respondents who were married was also high in DWRS. Ninety-one percent were married; 3% were widowed; 3% were separated or divorced; and 3% had never been married.

DSLS took its respondents from the same geographic region as did DWRS, and the distribution of respondents according to their marital status was quite similar. In DSLS 91% were married, 6% widowed, 2% separated or divorced, and 2% never married.

Education

Education is an important variable because it is a good indicator of socioeconomic status, and the relationship between the socioeconomic status and retirement is of particular interest in this research. Table 2.1 presents the educational level of the respondents in the analyses.

The fact that the respondents were all born in the early years of the twentieth century is reflected in their educational levels. In only three data sets, OLS, PSID, and DSLS, do more than half of the respondents have a high school education or more. OLS respondents have the highest levels of education, as more than a third have more than a college degree, and nearly 54% have at least a college degree. This is because the township where the research was undertaken includes a college campus. DWRS also has a high percentage with postgraduate education, as 33% possess education beyond the baccalaureate level. The distribution of education levels in DWRS is bimodal. While there is a large group at the upper end of the spectrum, 57% did not finish high school. Subjects for DWRS were selected from industry and academe, thus accounting for this rather unusual distribution.

MSAW has a very positively skewed education distribution. Nearly 80% have less than a high school education, while only 1%

completed college and virtually no one participated in any post-graduate education. This reflects the educational levels of auto workers. The distributions of RHS and NLS are quite similar because they are nationally representative samples. Between 57 and 69% lack high school educations. NLS and PSID had an oversampling of blacks and poor persons, which explains their higher proportions in the lower education levels.

Retirement Rates

The percentage of respondents who retired during the study is a particularly important statistic for several reasons. First, in the analyses of the predictors of retirement the major dependent variable is whether or not the respondent retired. The second major focus of the research was on the consequences of retirement. In these analyses, retirement status is the critical independent variable. A third analysis dealt with adjustment to retirement. In these analyses only those persons who have retired are included in the sample to be analyzed. Therefore the percent retired determines the sample size.

Three data sets had high levels of retirement: RHS, NLS, and PSID each had more than 80% of the respondents retired during the course of the study. In each of those cases all of the respondents were more than 65 years of age by the end of the study.

Three other data sets fall into the middle category with between 60 and 75% of the respondents retired. In DWRS and MSAW 75% of the respondents retired, and in DSLS the percentage retiring was 60%. These lower percentages are accounted for by the younger ages of the samples.

The final data set, OLS, falls into the low category. Only 37% of those present at Time 1 had retired by the second wave of the study (the final wave which we considered). The low retirement rate reflects the youth of the respondent (many were less than 65) and the fact that there were only two years between the first and second waves.

We now turn to the models to be examined and the statistical tests employed in the analyses.

METHODS FOR STATISTICAL MODELS AND TESTS

All of the analyses presented are applications of general linear statistical models and the techniques used to analyze such models. The particular statistical method to be used was based, essentially, upon two criteria: (1) whether the measurement of the independent and especially the dependent variables was categorical (qualitative) or continuous (quantitative); (2) whether the independent variables were modeled as predictors of the particular criterion variable, or were measuring characteristics to be used to discriminate certain groups or categories. In most cases the dependent variable was treated as more or less continuously measured, and the purpose of the analysis was to find the "best" set of predictors and/or to explain the relationship of the independent variables to the criterion response. Under these conditions, standard multiple regression models and statistical tests of significance were used. However, in some instances, the dependent variable was measured as discrete categories (representing certain groups, characteristics, or the occurrence of a particular event) such as objective and subjective retirement, early retirement, and reasons for retirement. Other appropriate methods were used for these analyses.

When the dependent variable was a continuous measure, multiple regression models, using ordinary least squares estimation, were fit to the data. In the analysis of predictors of retirement, when there were enough significant predictors to group into theoretical types, the multiple regressions were done in steps to determine the amount of increase in variance explained by each group of predictors (controlling for the predictor variables in previous stages). The groups of variables were arranged in order of their theoretical sequence in a causal model. Both unstandardized and standardized partial regression coefficients will be presented to indicate the net effects of the different independent variables in the equation at each stage of the model building process. The total variance explained by the variables in the equation (after adjusting for the number of observations and the number of parameters estimated) will be presented as an adjusted R^2.

For the analysis of the consequences of retirement, multiple regressions were done to build prediction equations for the possible outcomes dependent upon retirement. Preretirement levels of the dependent measure were entered into the models along with other Time 1 variables which significantly increased the explained variance of the outcome. The last stage of the model building process added (as the final independent variable in the equation) the retirement variable to determine whether there was any additional explained variance. This two-stage regression model building process was employed for all outcome measures considered as consequences of retirement.

Thus, the use of multiple regression analyses allowed the building of the "best," most parsimonious prediction equations, based upon which variables ought to be important according to theory, as well as any causal ordering that may be implied. We could assess both the relative predictive power of individual variables and the total explanatory power of the sets of independent variables in the equations.

Special problems arise, unfortunately, when the dependent variable is measured qualitatively, and particularly if it is a binary response (dichotomous) variable.

1. Non-normal Error Terms. Since for a binary dependent variable the error terms can take on only two values, clearly the normal error regression model is not appropriate.

2. Nonconstant Error Variance. The error terms do not have equal variances when the dependent variable is a dichotomy. Hence ordinary least squares will no longer be optimal for the estimation of the regression parameters.

3. Constraints on the Response Function. When the dependent variable is measured as a (0, 1) dichotomy, the response function represents probabilities (i.e., the probability of becoming retired); therefore the mean responses should be constrained between 0 and 1. A linear response function (such as a linear regression function) may fall outside the constraint limits within the range of the independent variables in the scope of the model.

As for the first problem, even though the error terms are not normally distributed, when the dependent variable is a binary response, the estimated regression coefficients (by ordinary least squares) are still approximately normal when the sample size is large. However, because of the second problem, unequal error variances, the estimated coefficients do not have the minimum variance property required. Thus the estimated coefficients are inefficient. An alternative approach is to use weighted least squares, which provide efficient estimates when the error variances are unequal. It has been shown, though, that under certain general conditions, if the mean responses on the dependent variable range between about 0.2 and 0.8 (for the scope of the model) there is little to be gained from weighted least squares (Cox, 1970). The last issue, that of constraints on the response function, could be handled by either ensuring that the fitted response function does not fall below 0 or above 1 within the range of the data (something that is not always easy in practice), or alternatively and perhaps more appropriately, by using a statistical model which meets the constraints automatically.

One such statistical model, which was used in these analyses and which is appropriate for relating a qualitative dependent variable to other explanatory variables, is the logistic regression model. This model satisfies the problems of a binary dependent variable discussed above (Walker & Duncan, 1967; Cox, 1970). For a dichotomous (binary) dependent variable the logistic regression model relates the probability of a positive response to any number of independent explanatory variables, whether measured quantitatively or qualitatively.

The logistic regression procedure calculates maximum likelihood estimates for the parameters of a model that expresses the natural log of the odds of an event as a simple linear model. The model may contain any number of independent variables. In the logistic regression analyses presented, the antilog of the estimated regression coefficient is computed for each explanatory variable. This coefficient (indicated by AC) estimates how much a change of 1 unit in the independent variable multiplies the odds of a positive response on the dependent criterion, holding the effects of the other variables in the equation constant. The overall fit of the logistic model is assessed by R. The R statistic is analogous to the multiple correlation coefficient in ordinary least squares regression after a correction is made for the number of parameters estimated in the particular equation. Individual R statistics are computed for each independent variable in the equation. The R values range between -1 and +1 and provide a measure of the relative contribution of each variable to the fit of the model. The sign of the individual R's corresponds to the direction of the multiplicative effect for the variable. Therefore a variable that lowers the odds of the event will have a negative R value and one that increases the odds will have a positive R value.

When the problem under discussion is one of classification, or discrimination, of given characteristics into one of two (or several) different populations, the logistic regression model is often preferred over linear discriminant function analysis (Press

& Wilson, 1978). One advantage of using the logistic model for discriminant analysis is that it is relatively robust with regard to any underlying assumptions about the distribution of the explanatory variates. In particular, the logistic formulation results not only from assuming that the explanatory variables are multivariate normally distributed with equal covariance matrices, but also from assuming that they are independent and dichotomous variables, or that some are multivariate normal and some dichotomous (Anderson, 1972). The linear discriminant analysis approach is strictly applicable only when the underlying variables are jointly normal with equal covariance matrices, an assumption that is often unlikely to be satisfied in application. Another possible problem with discriminant function estimators, under non-normality, is that they will tend not to be consistent and may be less efficient than corresponding logistic regression maximum likelihood estimators. Thus Halperin, Blackwelder, and Verter (1971) conclude that the "use of the maximum likelihood method would be preferable, whenever practical, in situations where the normality assumptions are violated, especially when many of the independent variables are qualitative."

Press and Wilson (1978) present detailed theoretical arguments for using logistic regression (with MLE estimators) instead of using linear discriminant analysis for both the classification problem and the problem of relating a qualitative dependent variable to explanatory variables. The authors found logistic regression outperforming classical linear discriminant analysis in two empirical studies of non-normal classification problems; however, it was "not by a large amount." They conclude that "it is unlikely that the two methods will give markedly different results, or yield substantially different linear functions unless there is a large proportion of observations whose x-values lie in regions of the factor space with linear logistic response probabilities near zero or one." Thus there seems to be a place for the use of discriminant function analysis, especially when the discriminating variables are more or less quantitative measures.

In the analysis of reasons for retirement and the analyses related to return to work we present the results of linear multiple discriminant analysis. In both analyses the explanatory variables are quantitative measures, and while there still exists the possibility that the normality assumption may be violated, we do not feel that the loss of efficiency is serious, nor that the substance of the results would be very different if alternative methods were used. In the analysis of the reasons for retirement we perform the multiple discriminant analysis using a canonical correlation approach. In practice, canonical correlation is used to simultaneously analyze multiple independent and dependent variables. When the dependent variables are categorical, or a set of 0-1 dummy variables representing groups, canonical correlation analysis is a mathematical identity with multiple discriminant analysis (Tatsuoka, 1971). The coefficients from the canonical correlation analysis are standardized partial regression coefficients that are analogous to the standardized coefficients produced by a multiple regression analysis. Therefore the relative discriminating power of the individual independent variables may be ascertained by examination of the individual coefficients. The canonical correlations between the independent variables and the dummy variables representing the groups (based on reason for retirement) indicate the overall discriminating power of the independent measures.

DIFFERENCES BETWEEN SUBGROUPS

One final methodological issue concerns the fitting of separate regression models to different subgroups in the data. For example, in our analysis of gender and race differences we have chosen to fit regression equations separately for each subpopulation, in order to assess the relative differences between the groups. While certain statistical tests exist for testing whether there is any difference in the regression coefficients between groups [these tests are usually referred to as Chow (1960) type tests], the results of such tests are greatly affected by the sample sizes of the separate groups and by the variances and degree of collinearity of the predetermined variables (Hanushek & Jackson, 1977). In addition, as a test of equality of sets of coefficients in two regressions, the Chow test assumes that the error variances are equal for the two regressions. There is evidence that the test may be inaccurate if this is not the case, in the sense that the true level of significance may not equal the nominal level of significance. The results may be further biased if the two sample sizes and the two variances are very different (Schmidt & Sickles, 1977). In several of our data sets (such as RHS and NLS) there is great inequality in the sample sizes of the subgroups of interest. In the RHS, there are over 10 times as many whites as blacks. A preliminary test of the differences between blacks and whites in the regression coefficients for the predictors of retirement tended to produce confusing results since the blacks in the sample were overwhelmed by the large sample size of the whites, and there appeared to be no significant interactions between race and other predictors. However, the results of separate regression equations revealed differences not only in magnitude of effect, but in the direction of the effect as well. The standard errors for the blacks were generally larger, due in part to the small sample size for the blacks, and therefore the regression coefficients were often not statistically significant, even when we had expected to find the results significant. Had the sample size for the blacks been larger, we may assume that the standard errors would have been smaller; and any test for an interaction would have smaller standard errors of the differences between the regression coefficients. Given the problems of relative sample sizes, and the possible effects on any tests for regression differences, we have chosen to examine the regression models separately for our analyses of important subgroup differences.

In summary, our use of multiple data sets and the most appropriate methods for multivariate analysis allow us to analyze the causes and consequences of retirement comprehensively, yet efficiently.

3
Predictors of Retirement

Most of the previous research on why people retire has been limited to cross-sectional and retrospective data (Atchley, 1976; Palmore, 1971; Sheppard, 1976). There has been little multivariate analysis of the predictors of retirement based on longitudinal data. A few studies examined bivariate relationships between prior characteristics of the individual and retirement at a later time, but the effects of other factors were not examined or controlled (Burkhauser, 1979; Parnes, 1981; Streib & Schneider, 1971). There also have been a few multivariate analyses of *plans* to retire, but plans to retire are often quite different from actual retirement (Barfield & Morgan, 1969, 1978; Morgan, 1980; Parnes & Nestel, 1971). Our literature search found only two multivariate analyses of the predictors of actual retirement and both used multiple classification analysis (MCA), which has serious limits when used with a dichotomous dependent variable and may produce biased results (Bixby, 1976).

The basic purpose of this chapter is to answer the question, "What factors best predict retirement?" Our study differs from earlier research in that it uses (1) multiple data sets; (2) multiple definitions of retirement; (3) longitudinal data (allowing prospective analysis of predictors); (4) multivariate analysis that simultaneously controls for all significant variables; and (5) statistical techniques that permit unbiased analyses of dichotomous dependent variables.

An earlier version of this chapter has appeared in the *Journal of Gerontology*, 1982, *37*, 733–742. Used by permission.

PREVIOUS STUDIES OF PREDICTORS

Parnes and Nestel used MCA to examine the predictors of early retirement among men aged 60 to 64 in 1971 in the National Longitudinal Survey (NLS) based on their characteristics in 1966 (reported in Bixby, 1976). Retirement was subjectively defined by the respondent's statement that he was "already retired." It should be noted that this method does not include some men as early retirees who would later retire before age 65. (Our analysis of early retirement in the NLS includes all men who retired before age 76.) They found only four statistically significant predictors of early retirement, listed in order of importance: index of work commitment, health-related work limitations, second-pension coverage (controlled for length of service), and job satisfaction.

Bixby (1976) also used MCA to predict retirement among men aged 62 to 67 in 1973 in the Retirement History Study (RHS) who were wage or salary workers in 1969. The self-employed were excluded. (Our analysis of the RHS includes self-employed.) Health-related work limitation was found to be a much stronger predictor of early retirement (those retired by age 65) than any of seven other factors. For men aged 66 to 67, health-related work limitation was a less important predictor and about equally important as coverage by a second pension. Occupation and attitude toward retirement were next in importance, and the other four factors tested were relatively unimportant. However, tests of statistical significance were not reported.

THEORETICAL MODEL

The previous research suggests five groups of important predictors of retirement: demographic characteristics, socioeconomic status, health, job characteristics, and attitudes toward work and retirement. Figure 3.1 shows a simplified theoretical model of how these predictors affect retirement. Demographic variables are assumed to come first in the causal chain and to have both direct effects on retirement and indirect effects through the other variables. Socioeconomic variables are assumed to come second and to have direct effects on retirement as well as indirect effects through the subsequent variables. Similarly, health and job characteristics are assumed to have both direct effects on retirement and indirect

FIGURE 3.1. Theoretical model of factors predicting retirement.

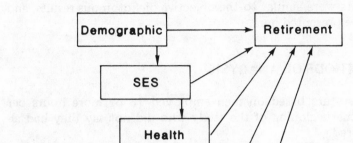

effects through subsequent variables. Finally, attitudes are assumed to be the result of all the other variables and to have only direct effects on retirement. We expect that there may actually be complex interaction patterns and nonlinear relationships between these variables, but our primary purpose is to measure the total effects of these variables on retirement, to determine their relative predictive powers, and to develop the most parsimonious and powerful prediction equations possible from these data sets.

A basic question to be examined is the relative importance of structural variables (demographic, socioeconomic, and job characteristics) as opposed to subjective variables (self-rated health, attitudes). Parnes and Nestel, as well as Bixby (1976), found that subjective variables (index of work commitment, self-rated health limitations, job satisfaction) were more important than structural variables for early retirement. However, for "on-time" retirees, Bixby (1976) found that structural and subjective variables were about equally important. Earlier cross-sectional and retrospective studies (Palmore, 1971) found subjective variables (especially self-rated health) to be of primary importance.

We will compare the results of using two definitions of retirement: the objective dichotomous definition and the contin-

uous definition (amount of employment). The subjective definition results were similar to the objective dichotomous results, and
will not be presented here.

TWO METHODS OF ANALYSIS

All analyses are based on men employed 16 or more hours per
week at the beginning of the study who did not say they had already retired.

For the analyses of age at retirement and amount of employment, standard multiple regression analysis (ordinary least squares)
was used because the dependent variables are continuous (see
Chapter 2). When there were enough significant predictors to
group into types, the multiple regressions were done in stages to
determine the amount of increase in variance explained by each
group of predictors [with the predictors in previous stage(s) statistically controlled]. The groups of variables were arranged in
order of their theoretical primacy in a causal model: demographic
variables, socioeconomic status (SES), health, job characteristics,
and attitudes (Figure 3.1). The tables in this chapter (3.1 to 3.7)
present only those predictors that significantly increase the variance explained at the .05 level. In the multiple regression tables

TABLE 3.1
Significant Predictors of Objective Retirement
in the RHS (Logistic Regression)[a]

1969 Predictors	Demographic		SES		Health		Job Characteristics	
	AC	R	AC	R	AC	R	AC	R
Age	1.21	.06	1.24	.07	1.25	.08	1.42	.11
Education			.95	-.02	.96	.00	.92	-.08
Occupation			.86	-.10	.86	-.10	.86	-.09
Health limits					1.16	.04	1.18	.07
Years on job							1.02	.05
Years worked since 21							.89	-.07
Pension plan							1.67	.07
Mandatory retirement							2.62	.11
Total R		.06		.17		.18		.31

[a]*Men aged 66 to 69 in 1975 (N = 877).*

TABLE 3.2
Significant Predictors of Objective Retirement
in the NLS (Logistic Regression)[a]

1966 Predictors	AC	Variable R	Total R
Number of children under 18	.89	-.02	.01
Education	.91	-.11	.19
Poverty ratio	.999	-.10	.24
Employed by others	2.74	.16	.29
Retirement attitude	1.22	.09	.31

[a]*Men aged 66 to 69 in 1976 (N = 606).*

the *b* values are the unstandardized regression coefficients, and
the beta values are the standardized coefficients. The adjusted
R^2 shows the variance explained, adjusted for the number of variables and cases.

Objective retirement (ages 65 and over) and early retirement
(ages under 65) are dichotomous variables, and for these variables
logistic regression analysis was used (see Chapter 2). The logistic
regression procedure calculates maximum likelihood estimates for

TABLE 3.3
Significant Predictors of Annual Hours Worked
in the RHS (Multiple Regression)[a]

1969 Predictors	Demographic		SES		Health		Job	
	b	beta	*b*	beta	*b*	beta	*b*	beta
Age	-34.8	-.04	-39.4	-.05	-40.4	-.05	-64.7	-.08
Number dependents	96.09	.10	97.0	.12	95.3	.10	98.1	.10
Married	-156.8	-.05	-156.2	-.05	-154.6	-.05	-217.7	-.07
Education			29.8	.11	28.5	.11	30.8	.12
Work limits					-99.0	-.04	-181.3	-.07
Years worked since 21							15.4	.14
Self-employed							643.1	.26
Mandatory retirement							-400.5	-.19
Adjusted R^2		.01		.02		.02		.18

[a]*Men aged 66 to 69 in 1975 (N = 759).*

TABLE 3.4
**Significant Predictors of Annual Hours Worked
in the NLS (Multiple Regression)[a]**

1966 Predictors	Demographic		SES		Job		Attitudes	
	b	beta	b	beta	b	beta	b	beta
Age	-100.6	-.13	-111.4	-.14	-118.7	-.15	-110.5	-.14
Race	-20.3	-.01	155.9	.08	226.4	.11	207.2	.10
Poverty ratio			0.5	.22	0.4	.19	0.4	.19
Occupation			3.5	.10	5.3	.15	5.3	.15
Self-employed					343.1	.16	324.2	.15
Core industry					-192.7	-.11	-172.6	-.10
Mandatory retirement					-228.2	-.12	-215.4	-.11
Area unemployment					-96.3	-.09	-93.7	-.09
Retirement attitude							-62.1	-.12
Adjusted R^2	.02		.07		.16		.17	

[a]*Men aged 66 to 69 in 1976 (N = 613).*

TABLE 3.5
**Significant Predictors of Early Retirement
in the RHS (Logistic Regression)[a]**

1969 Predictors	Demographic		SES		Health		Job Characteristics	
	AC	R	AC	R	AC	R	AC	R
Race	.62	.00	.55	-.03	.49	-.04	.43	-.06
Married	.70	.00	.64	-.03	.59	-.04	.54	-.06
Income adequacy			.96	.00	.96	.00	.83	.07
Health rating					.64	-.10	.64	-.10
Self-employed							.47	-.07
Years worked since 21							.98	-.05
Mandatory retirement							2.08	.12
Total R	.00		.00		.11		.17	

[a]*Men aged 66 in 1975 (N = 713). Only age 66 was analyzed because the data do not
allow certain identification of early retirees among the other age groups.*

TABLE 3.6
Significant Predictors of Early Retirement
in the NLS (Logistic Regression)[a]

1966 Predictors	AC	Variable R	Total R
Age	.85	-.08	.07
Education	.92	-.13	.14
Health rating	.72	-.09	.16
Pension	1.63	.08	.20
Rural	.81	-.06	.21
Retirement attitude	1.19	.11	.24

[a]*Men aged 65 to 69 in 1976 (N = 805).*

the parameters of a model that expresses the log of the odds of an event as a simple linear model. In the logistic regression tables the AC is the antilogged coefficient that estimates how changes in the independent variables multiply the odds of retirement, holding other variables in the equation constant. The overall fit of the model is assessed by R. The R statistic is analogous to the multiple correlation coefficient in ordinary least squares regression after a correction is made for the number of parameters estimated. Individual R statistics are also presented for each indepen-

TABLE 3.7
Significant Predictors of Age at Retirement
in the NLS (Multiple Regression)[a]

1966 Predictors	Demographic		SES		Health		Job		Attitudes	
	b	beta	b	beta	b	beta	b	beta	b	beta
Rural	.34	.11	.55	.17	.59	.18	.45	.14	.40	.12
Wage ($1000)			.06	.11	.04	.07	.08	.16	.08	.16
Occupation			.02	.18	.02	.18	.02	.16	.02	.15
Health limits					-1.16	-.18	-1.13	-.17	-1.02	-.16
Mandatory retirement							-1.11	-.18	-1.14	-.18
Core industry							-.80	-.14	-.64	-.11
Job attitude									-.34	-.21
Retirement attitude									.59	.14
Adjusted R^2		.01		.06		.09		.14		.19

[a]*Men aged 68 to 69 in 1976 (N = 295).*

dent variable in the model. R values range between −1 and +1 and provide a measure of the contribution of each variable to the fit of the model.

In Tables 3.2 and 3.6 there were not enough significant predictors to group into types so only the final AC and R are presented, but the increases in Total R are presented in the third column. The same variables were used in all analyses (if the data were available), but only the significant predictors are shown. For example, in Table 3.5 mandatory retirement also was tested but found to be a nonsignificant predictor net of the other variables.

FINDINGS

Predictors of Objective Retirement (Dichotomous Definition)

Looking first at our largest national study, the RHS, we see that the only significant demographic predictor of objective retirement is age (Table 3.1). This shows the continuing importance of age in motivating or forcing retirement even among those four years older than the "normal" retirement age (ages 66 to 69).

Note that although age is related to health and various job characteristics, it becomes an even stronger predictor of retirement when all other significant predictors are entered in the equation (final two columns). In the NLS age was not significant, but number of children under age 18 was, although the R value was quite low (.01, Table 3.2). Because number of children under age 18 has a strong negative correlation with age, this may partially explain why older men retire more: they have fewer dependents to support. It is noteworthy that none of the other demographic variables tested (race, marital status, region, rural-urban residence) were significant predictors.

The SES predictors (education, occupation, poverty ratio) were of major importance, increasing the R value by 11 points in the RHS and by 23 points in the NLS. Higher SES men apparently had more opportunities and incentives to continue working past age 65. Health variables were not significant in the NLS and increased the R value in the RHS by only one point.

Job characteristics were also of major importance, increasing the R value by 13 points in the RHS. Having a job covered by a pension plan and being subject to mandatory retirement were especially important in the RHS, and being employed by others (which is closely related to having a job covered by a pension plan and mandatory retirement) is the strongest single predictor in the NLS. It alone almost tripled the odds of retirement in the NLS (AC = 2.74) as did mandatory retirement in the RHS (AC = 2.62).

Retirement attitudes were not significant in the RHS, and they increased the R value by only two points in the NLS. It is reassuring that although somewhat different variables became significant predictors in the two large national samples, the total R values were identical (.31).

The analyses of objective retirement in the other studies found fewer significant predictors because of smaller samples, but the patterns were basically the same except for differences accounted for by the differing types of samples (e.g., age was more important in the DSLS because of the wider age range).

In summary, these analyses show that structural factors, such as SES and job characteristics that increased the incentives or necessity of retirement, were stronger predictors of objective retirement (among all those over 65) than were the subjective characteristics of health self-rating and retirement attitude.

Predictors of Amount of Employment (Continuous Definition)

This is a reverse measure of retirement; the fewer hours worked per year the more retired a person is. For this reason it should be kept in mind that in order to make Tables 3.3 and 3.4 comparable with the other tables, the signs on the bs and betas need to be reversed. For example, Table 3.4 shows that age is a negative predictor of annual hours worked; older men work *less*. In terms of retirement, it is a positive predictor; older men are *more* retired. Amount of employment has the major advantage of being a continuous variable that allows finer distinctions (among the partially retired) than the gross dichotomy of retired or not.

Three demographic variables (age, number of dependents, and being married) were statistically significant in the RHS, but all together explained only 1% of the variance (Table 3.4). It is interesting that more dependents *increase* the amount of work (presumably because more dependents increase the need for earnings), but being married *decreases* the amount worked (perhaps because the wife is a source of income, through earnings and/or increased benefits under Social Security). The effects of those two predictors were so small that they were not statistically significant in the NLS (Table 3.4). Instead, race was statistically significant and shows an interesting reversal when SES is controlled: in the bivariate correlation, race is negatively related to amount worked (meaning that nonwhites worked less) but becomes a positive predictor when SES is controlled (meaning that when prior income and occupation are controlled, nonwhites work more). This illustrates the importance of multivariate analysis that shows the independent effect of predictors when other significant predictors are controlled.

The SES variable, education, is significant in the RHS (the more educated work more), but it increases the variance explained by only 1%. Similarly in the NLS the SES variables of poverty ratio and occupation are significant predictors (men with higher income and occupation work more) but together increase the variance by only 5%.

As for health variables, only in the RHS was work limitation significant, and it increased the variance explained by only .001. This is in sharp contrast to the importance of health in early retirement and age at retirement.

In both studies the major predictors are job characteristics, with self-employment being the strongest. It alone increases the annual hours worked by 643 in the RHS and by 324 in the NLS. Mandatory retirement is also a powerful predictor in both studies, decreasing the hours worked by 400 in the RHS and by 215 in the NLS. Years worked since age 21 also is a fairly strong predictor in the RHS; apparently men who have been healthier and/or more committed to their jobs and so worked more steadily continue to work more in old age. In the NLS working in a core industry (construction or production) *decreased* work in old age, perhaps because of better pension benefits and/or less attractive jobs in the core industry. Persons living in higher unemployment areas also worked less, presumably because of the difficulty of getting employment.

There were no significant attitude predictors in the RHS, and retirement attitudes in the NLS increased the variance explained by only 1%.

The other studies showed similar patterns but had fewer significant predictors because of their smaller sizes. There were a few additional significant predictors. In the PSID having had a different job in the last five years decreased the annual hours worked by 125 hours. Whereas this is a measure of job instability, this relationship is similar to the relationship in the RHS between years worked since 21 and amount of employment. In the OLS fewer symptoms of stress predicted more work (as expected), but with stress controlled poorer health predicted *more* work. This is an unexpected finding, but it may result from the greater need of persons in poorer health for the continued medical care benefits and/or earnings of continued work. In contrast, the DSLS found that better health predicted more work. These contradictory findings may reflect the small size of the samples and the borderline significance of health variables as predictors of amount of work.

The DSLS also found two significant attitude predictors: Those who said they would "work if I didn't have to" and those who said they "prefer work to leisure" actually did work more at the end of the study.

The DWRS found that church attendance was a significant positive predictor of amount worked (per week). This may indicate that the more religious have a stronger work ethic. The DWRS also found that greater seniority on the job predicted less work; perhaps those with more seniority have better pension benefits.

In summary, the amount worked at the end of the studies was predicted mainly by job characteristics such as being self-employed, not subject to mandatory retirement, and not employed in a core industry. In the large national studies demographic, SES, health, and attitude predictors all together explained less of the variance than the job characteristics. This indicates that structural factors are more important predictors of amount worked (or retired) than all the individual and subjective factors put together.

Predictors of Early Retirement

The significant predictors of early retirement (objective retirement before age 65) presented a somewhat different pattern from the predictors of retirement among men over 65 (Tables 3.5 and 3.6). In the RHS, the demographic and SES variables combined produced a total R of less than .005. In the NLS age produced an R of .07 because younger men had more years in which to retire early. In both studies health variables became more important predictors than in the previous analyses, and job characteristics became relatively less important. In the NLS retirement attitude became more important. The other studies showed similar results, although fewer variables were significant.

Thus, in comparison with normal age retirement, early retirement appears to be more influenced by the subjective factors of self-rated health and attitudes.

Predictors of Age at Retirement

Demographic factors were also unimportant in predicting age at retirement. Only rural residence was a significant predictor, and it explained only 1% of the variance in the NLS (Table 3.7). Rural residence probably predicts later retirement because farm and rural jobs allow and encourage continued work. In this sense rural residence could be considered a job characteristic.

The SES variables (annual wages and occupation) were strong positive predictors of later age at retirement. This again reflects greater opportunities and incentives to continue working in higher SES groups.

Health limitations were again a relatively strong predictor of earlier retirement, as were the job characteristics of mandatory retirement and core industry. Both job attitudes and retirement attitudes were also strong predictors of age at retirement.

Thus, age at retirement, which covers early and later retirement, is predicted by a balanced mixture of SES, health, job, and attitude variables.

DISCUSSION

A major finding of these analyses is that the predictors of retirement vary markedly depending on how retirement is defined and measured. If retirement is defined objectively as working less than full-time and receiving a pension, then the strongest predictors among those over age 65 are structural factors such as SES and job characteristics that increase the incentives or necessity of retirement. Health and attitudes are relatively unimportant. All our analyses show that health variables were almost useless as predictors of objective retirement among men over age 65. We suspect that the earlier cross-sectional studies that found poor health to be related strongly to retirement among those over age 65 were biased by retrospective and social desirability distortions. Once a person has retired for whatever voluntary or involuntary reasons, poor health is a socially acceptable explanation, and therefore its importance may be exaggerated retrospectively.

In contrast to the dichotomous measure of retirement, if retirement is operationalized as a continuous variable and measured (negatively) by amount employed past age 65, the job characteristics are more important predictors than all the others added together. Thus, demographic and SES variables are more important predictors of the dichotomous measure of retirement, while job characteristics are more important predictors of the continuous measure of retirement.

In contrast, to the predictors of retirement at normal ages, health variables and attitudes *were* important predictors for early retirement and for age at retirement (which is another way of analyzing who retires early or late). But SES and job characteristics also are important predictors of early retirement and age at retirement. Thus, subjective factors (such as health assessments and attitudes) were equally important to structural factors in predicting early retirement and age at retirement.

These conclusions are generally compatible with the findings of the other prospective studies (Bixby, 1976), although their methods and samples were more limited than those used in this analysis. Our theoretical explanation of this convergence of findings would be as follows. At ages under 65, retirement is neither expected nor forced by mandatory retirement. Therefore early retirement is more influenced by subjective factors such as self-perceptions of health, attitudes toward work and retirement, and perceived adequacy of retirement income. However, at ages over 65, most workers are pressured to retire by mandatory retirement policies and expectations of employers, fellow workers, friends, and family. Therefore, only the few who are self-employed or in jobs not subject to mandatory retirement (structural factors) are able to continue much employment.

This interpretation is also compatible with Parnes' conclusion (1981) that few men are actually forced to retire by mandatory retirement rules. The majority of men choose to retire early, either because they perceive their health to be limiting their work or because they have adequate retirement incomes. Among the minority who choose to work until age 65, most choose to retire soon thereafter because of increasing pressures to retire exerted by employers, fellow workers, and family. This is especially true of those with adequate pensions and/or failing health. Thus, there are few left who are literally forced to retire by mandatory retirement rules.

As for the model shown in Figure 3.1, our findings indicate that all five types of variables are significant predictors, net of all others, for each definition of retirement in at least one national study. However, in contrast to earlier cross-sectional studies, we found health to be relatively unimportant in predicting retirement among men over age 65.

Retirement is usually thought to have serious consequences for older workers. It clearly affects the way elders spend their time, the amount of their income, and who they interact with. It also has been assumed to impair their physical and mental health, self-esteem, happiness, and life satisfaction. As a result, the consequences of retirement is one of the most researched topics in gerontology.

Most of the research on the consequences of retirement, however, has been limited to cross-sectional data (Atchley, 1976; Bengtson, 1969; Bixby et al., 1975; Cottrell & Atchley, 1969; Epstein & Murray, 1967; Havighurst et al., 1969; Nadelson, 1969; Shanas, 1972; Shanas et al., 1968; Simpson & McKinney, 1966; Thompson, 1973, 1974). Such studies are somewhat inconsistent, but they often find that retirees, compared with nonretirees, have substantially less income, more physical and mental illness, lower self-esteem, less happiness, and less life satisfaction. As a result, many fear that when they retire they will get sick, senile, depressed and soon die. The main weakness of such studies is that they do not control for selection effects: Retirees may have had these negative characteristics *before* they retired. Only longitudinal studies that have information on preretirement characteristics can control these selection effects.

There have been a few published longitudinal analyses of the consequences of retirement, but these usually control for only one or two preretirement characteristics before retirement (Haynes et al., 1978; Morgan, 1981; Parnes, 1981; Streib & Schneider,

An earlier version of this chapter has appeared in the *Journal of Gerontology*, 1984, *39*, 109–116. Used by permission.

1971). In reality there are usually several factors that influence the outcomes in question. Furthermore, different results may be found depending on how retirement is defined.

The basic purpose of this chapter is to answer the question, "What are the consequences of retirement when relevant preretirement characteristics are controlled?" The study differs from earlier research in that it used (1) longitudinal data, (2) multivariate analyses that simultaneously control for all significant preretirement characteristics, (3) multiple data sets, and (4) multiple measures of retirement.

There are two major theories about the effects of retirement on the retiree: crisis and continuity theory. Crisis theory postulates that retirement has generally negative and degrading effects because occupational identity is the basic legitimizing role for workers in our society. Loss of this role through retirement implies inability to perform, which reduces self-respect and status, which leads to further withdrawal from social participation, which leads to isolation, illness, and decline in happiness and life satisfaction (Burgess, 1960; Miller, 1965; Rosow, 1962).

Continuity theory, in contrast, postulates that occupational identity is not the central role for many workers. Retirement has become a legitimate and desirable role with opportunities for the continuation of other roles and development of new leisure roles, which provides a continuation of self-esteem and status. Therefore, it postulates little or no long-term effects of retirement (Atchley, 1971a, 1976; Palmore, 1981).

Both these theories are too general and sweeping. Crisis theory is mistaken in assuming that occupational identity is necessarily the central and legitimizing role in our society. Many workers consider their job to be primarily a means of earning a living so they can carry out the roles more important to them. Retirement does not necessarily imply inability to perform; many retire voluntarily to take advantage of leisure opportunities. Retirement has become a respectable and often desirable role in our society.

On the other hand, continuity theory does not recognize that retirement may have significant effects on some outcomes for some workers in some situations. Almost all retirees experience a reduction in income, and most reduce their amount of employment. Some are forced to retire early or before they wish to retire because of disability or mandatory retirement. These retirees may experience severe negative consequences. On the other hand, some are happy to retire and may experience substantial positive effects.

Therefore, we propose that retirement will have differential effects depending on (1) the type of outcome, (2) the timing of retirement, and (3) the type of workers. Specifically, we hypothesize that retirement will usually have substantial effects only on those outcomes directly and necessarily linked to retirement, such as income and amount of employment, and that it will usually have little or no long-term effects on indirect outcomes such as health, activities, and attitudes. We also hypothesize that early retirement will have more negative effects than on-time retirement, for reasons discussed later. This chapter is an examination of these hypotheses. Later chapters will examine the hypothesis that retirement has differential effects for different types of workers (by gender, race, and socioeconomic status).

METHODS

All the analyses presented in this chapter were based on men employed 16 or more hours at the beginning who did not say they had already retired. (Separate analyses were done on women, and these results are presented in Chapter 8.)

Most of the consequences analyzed involved continuous variables, so multiple regression analysis (ordinary least squares) was used. A few of the consequences were dichotomous measures (e.g., receiving food stamps). For these consequences the results of the multiple regression analyses were compared with the results of logistic multiple regression analysis to detect any bias that might have occurred in the ordinary least squares model. The results were similar in all cases.

Most of the consequences analyzed were measured both at the beginning and end of the studies. This made it possible to control for preretirement levels of the variable used to test for consequences of retirement. In addition, we entered into the first stage of the multiple regression all other Time 1 variables that significantly increased the variance explained in the outcome. Then we entered in the second stage (as the final independent variable) the retirement measure to see if it significantly increased the variance explained and, if so, by how much (see Figure 4.1).

Tables 4.1 to 4.6 are summary tables for each of the six longitudinal studies that present the variance explained in each consequence by its significant predictors without the retirement measure (Column 1) and the increase in variance explained by the

FIGURE 4.1. Model for analysis of retirement process.

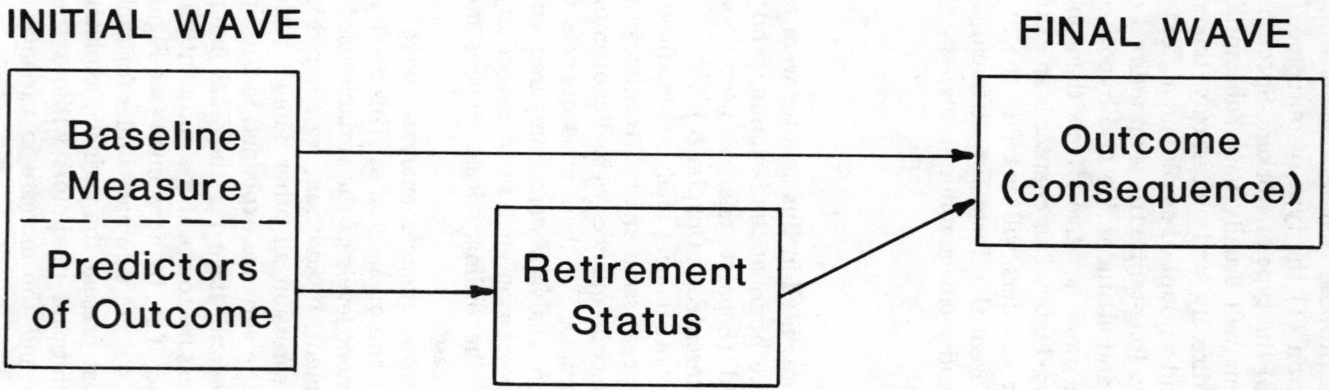

TABLE 4.1
Significant Consequences of Retirement among NLS Men

Consequences	Total R^2 without Retirement	R^2 Increase due to Retirement Measure		
		Objective	Continuous	Subjective
Income (−)	.19	.01	.02	.01
SSI(+)	.09	.01	.01	.01
Food stamps (+)	.13	.01	.01	.01
Living standard (−)	.12		.01	.01
Health limits (+)	.11	.06	.08	.02
Health factor (−)	.14	.04	.05	.05

Note: Consequences shown are those for which the increase in R^2 was significant at .05 level and the increase was greater than .005. Consequences tested but found not significant included poverty ratio, assets, leisure satisfaction, residence satisfaction, happiness, and internal orientation. Analyses were performed on data from 1477 men aged 62 to 69 in 1976. Positive or negative signs indicate positive or negative association with retirement.

TABLE 4.2
Significant Consequences of Retirement among RHS Men

Consequences	Total R^2 without Retirement	R^2 Increase due to Retirement Measure		
		Objective	Continuous	Subjective
Income adequacy (−)	.36	.02	.06	.04
Health factor (−)	.17	.01	.03	.02
Formal organizations (−)	.54		.01	.01
Extra-work interests (+)	.53			.01
Activity satisfaction (+ −)	.09		.02(+)	.01(−)
Life satisfaction (−)	.31		.01	
Retirement attitude (+)	.05	.04	.05	.07

Note: Consequences shown are those for which the increase in R^2 was significant at .05 level and was greater than .005. Consequences tested but found not significant included worry about finances, family, friends, and solitary-sedentary activities. Analyses were performed on data from 1468 men aged 64 to 69 in 1975. Positive or negative signs indicate positive or negative association with retirement.

TABLE 4.3
Significant Consequences of Retirement among PSID Men

Consequences	Total R^2 without Retirement	R^2 Increase due to Retirement Measure		
		Objective	Continuous	Subjective
Income (−)	.36	.05	.12	.08
Income adequacy (−)	.46	.02	.08	.02
Poverty ratio (−)	.48	.02	.05	.01
Health limits (+)	.08	.11	.08	.10

Note: Consequences shown are those for which the increase in R^2 was significant at .05 level. Consequences tested but found not significant included house value and rent. Analyses were performed on data from 288 men aged 62 to 69 in 1977. Positive or negative signs indicate positive or negative association with retirement.

TABLE 4.4
Significant Consequences of Retirement for DSLS Men

Consequences	Total R^2 without Retirement	R^2 Increase due to Retirement Measure		
		Objective	Continuous	Subjective
Income (−)	.39	.13	.17	.09
Health (−)	.22		.04	
Psychosomatic symptoms (+)	.24	.01	.03	.05
Solitary activity (+)	.08	.05	.02	.08
Self-care activity (+)	.14	.02	.04	
Time with friends (+)	.09	.03	.03	
Nonemployment work (+)	.12	.04	.08	.02
Church attendance (+)	.45	.02	.04	.07
Future orientation (−)	.09	.02		
Social value (+)	.32	.02	.04	
Usefulness (−)	.24	.12	.11	.15
Negative affect (+)	.12			.03

Note: Consequences shown are those for which the increase in R^2 was significant at .05 level. Consequences tested but found not significant included hours doing nothing, organizational activity, anomie, locus of control, age identification, life satisfaction, positive affect, and affect balance. Analyses were performed on data from 150 men aged 56 and over in 1976. Positive or negative signs indicate positive or negative association with retirement.

TABLE 4.5
Significant Consequences of Retirement among DWRS Men

| Consequences | Total R^2 without Retirement | R^2 Increase due to Retirement Measure | |
		Objective	Continuous
Health compared to others (+)	.06		.02
Friends seen (+)	.23		.02
Sense of autonomy (+)	.30	.04	

Note: Consequences shown are those for which the increase in R^2 was significant at .05 level. Consequences tested but found not significant included income, self-rated health, health limitations, health change, people seen frequently, usefulness, morale, and life satisfaction. Analyses were performed on data from 121 men aged 60 and over in 1966. Positive or negative signs indicate positive or negative association with retirement.

addition of the three different retirement measures. The second columns present the significant increases in variance explained by the objective measure of retirement, the third columns present the significant increases explained by the continuous measure, and the fourth columns present the significant increases explained by the subjective measure. Thus, each cell in Tables 4.1 to 4.6 represents the results of a two-stage multiple regression analysis.

Analysis of the few outcome measures that had no Time 1 scores could not, of course, include a control for initial levels on

TABLE 4.6
Significant Consequences of Retirement among OLS Men

Consequences	Total R^2 without Retirement	R^2 Increase due to Retirement Measure Subjective
Health (−)	.09	.01
Social withdrawal (+)	.36	.04

Note: Consequences shown are those for which the increase in R^2 was significant at .05 level. Consequences tested but found not significantly related to retirement included income adequacy, functional health, goals, retirement attitude, morale, activity, and confidence. None of the objective nor continuous measures of retirement showed any significant consequences. Analyses were performed on data from 67 men aged 62 or more in 1977. Positive or negative signs indicate positive or negative association with retirement.

that measure. The inclusion of other significant Time 1 predictors as control variables, however, provides a partial control for initial levels insofar as the other variables would be associated with the (unmeasured) initial levels of the outcome variable.

The footnote in each table lists those outcome measures that were tested but found to be not related significantly to retirement. These findings of *no* significant relationship, for outcomes thought to be consequences of retirement, are as important theoretically as those that were significantly related.

All variables are coded so that higher scores mean more of the variable or the positive end of the scale. Descriptions of these variables are in the Appendix.

Whereas correlation cannot prove causation, it should be understood that we use the terms "consequences" and "effects" in the sense that these correlations indicate possible or probable causal relationships. Causal inference is buttressed by the fact that the dependent variables are measured at a later time than the independent variables.

CONSEQUENCES

Four types of possible consequences of retirement were examined: income, health, activity, and attitudes.

Income. It is well known that income usually drops after retirement. The significant relationships between all three measures of retirement and income are confirmed by four of the six studies (Tables 4.1 through 4.4). It is surprising that two studies (DWRS and OLS) found no significant effects of retirement on income (after initial characteristics were controlled). The three large national studies found small to moderate effects of retirement on income. In the NLS, actual dollar amounts were recorded for income, and this made possible estimates of the net effects of retirement on income in dollars: a $2114 reduction following objective retirement and a $2406 reduction following subjective retirement. Whereas mean income was $8495 at the beginning of the NLS, a reduction of $2114 or $2406 would be a reduction of about 25% to 28%. The RHS data show a similar reduction in income (27%) after initial characteristics were controlled. This is a considerably smaller reduction than typically reported in cross-sectional studies.

Other financial effects of retirement (assets, living standard, house value or rent, and whether receiving food stamps or Supplementary Security Income) were even smaller than the effects on income.

Health. It is popularly believed that retirement often impairs health. Indeed, all the studies show significant net relationships between some measure of retirement and some measure of health. Some measures are not significantly related, however, and most of those that are show only modest increases in explained variance. If we omit the analyses in which there were no Time 1 scores (NLS and PSID), the increases ranged from .01 to .04.

Activity. By definition, the amount of employment activity is reduced by retirement, but an important question is whether retirement tends to increase, decrease, or have no effect on other types of activity. The RHS was the only national study with data on these activities; it showed small but significant *reductions* in activities in formal organizations but a small *increase* in extrawork interests (Table 4.2). It showed no significant effects of retirement on the other types of activity tested: social-family, social-friends, and solitary-sedentary activities. The DSLS showed that retirement tended to *increase* several types of activities: solitary leisure activity, self-care activity, time with friends, nonemployment work, and church attendance (Table 4.4). On the other hand, retirement had no significant effect on amount of organizational activity. Similarly, the DWRS showed an increase in number of friends seen but no effects on the number of other people seen (Table 4.5). In contrast, the OLS showed an increase in a measure of social withdrawal after retirement but no effects on the overall activity measure (Table 4.6).

Attitudes. There is continuing debate over whether and how retirement changes attitudes, especially happiness and life satisfaction. Our analyses showed mixed results. In the NLS none of the attitude measures (leisure satisfaction, residence satisfaction, happiness, locus of control) were significantly related to retirement. In the RHS life satisfaction has a slight negative relation to the continuous retirement measure but not to the other two measures (Table 4.2). Satisfaction with levels of activity also had a slight negative relation to the subjective retirement measure but a slight *positive* relation to the continuous retirement measure. As might be expected, attitude toward retirement was more positive among the retired. In the DSLS future orientation had a slight negative relation to the objective retirement measure but not to the other two (Table 4.4). Also in the DSLS feelings of own social value had *positive* relations to retirement, but the retired felt *less* useful and reported more *negative* affect (but only for the subjective measure of retirement). Anomie, locus of control, age identification, life satisfaction, positive affect, and affect balance had no significant relations to retirement in the DSLS. Similarly, the DWRS showed a greater sense of autonomy among the objectively retired but no relation between retirement and feelings of usefulness, morale, or life satisfaction (Table 4.5). The OLS also showed no significant relations between retirement and goals in life, retirement attitude, morale, or confidence.

Early Retirement

In view of these generally small and often inconsistent effects of retirement, we wondered if the effects might be stronger and clearer among those who retired early. Analyses in the national data sets for men under age 65 were repeated to see if early retirement had substantially different effects. We could not do this for the local studies because of the small numbers who retired early.

The effects of retirement among men under age 65 were generally similar to those among all the men, except for the following substantial differences. In the NLS the effects of early retirement on income were stronger (objective early retirement reduced income by $2917 under age 65 compared with $2114 for all men) as were the effects on satisfaction with living standard (greater decrease) and the proportion receiving Supplementary Security Income (greater increase). In addition, early retirement significantly decreased happiness and internal orientation, neither of which were significant effects among all men. It should be remembered that all these analyses controlled for initial health and other characteristics.

In the RHS early retirement also had stronger effects on income and life satisfaction (greater decreases) as well as stronger effects on health (greater decrease). Similarly, in the PSID early retirement had stronger effects on income and health (greater decreases).

Thus, all three national studies agreed that early retirement had stronger effects, especially in decreasing income and health.

DISCUSSION

Income. Given the well-known fact that income usually drops after retirement, it is surprising that the effects of retirement on income are usually small (reduced about one-fourth) once preretirement characteristics are controlled. Although cross-sectional analysis showed that objectively retired men had $4138 less than still-working men (1976 NLS data), controlling for initial characteristics reduced this effect to $2114, or by about one-half. RHS data showed that initial characteristics reduced the effect by about one-fourth. Thus, about one-fourth to one-half of the income differences between retired and working men is accounted for by preretirement differences. This can also be seen by the fact that in the NLS cross-sectional analysis, retirement alone accounts for about 3% of the variance in income, but when preretirement characteristics are controlled the net increase in variance explained by retirement reduces to about 1%. Similarly, in the RHS and the PSID the amount of variance explained by retirement alone is reduced by about one-half when preretirement characteristics are controlled. This helps explain why the net increases in income variance explained by retirement are so small and why this increase is not even significant in two of the studies. The same is true of the other financial effects of retirement.

Parnes' (1981) analysis of the NLS data reported reductions in income after retirement of 33% for blacks and 42% for whites, but prior characteristics and the reduction that would have occurred even if the men had continued to work were not controlled.

Health. A similar picture emerges for the health consequences. For example, objective retirement alone explains about 6% of the variance in the health variable in cross-sectional analysis (NLS data), but when initial differences are controlled, the net increase in variance explained by retirement is reduced to 4%. The question remains, however, does even this modest increase in explained variance mean that retirement tends to cause health deterioration? We believe it does not. There are two better explanations for this association between retirement and poorer health. First, although we attempted to control for initial levels of health, the health of some of those who later retired deteriorated between the time of the initial survey and the time of retirement (which was often several years). Therefore, this deterioration in health *before retirement* may have caused the retirement, rather than the retirement causing the deterioration in health. This interpretation is supported by the fact that voluntary retirees had no declines in health when compared to nonretirees (see Chapter 6). Secondly, men who have retired may be motivated to exaggerate their health limitations in order to justify their retirement. Since we do not have any objective measures of health, there is no way to test this hypothesis. It is certainly true that health does deteriorate after retirement for some men, but these cases may be balanced by others whose health improves after retirement because they are no longer subject to stressful, unhealthy, or dangerous work conditions. A recent review of the research concludes that there is no clear evidence for adverse effects of retirement on health (Minkler, 1981). The Boston VA study also found no adverse effects of retirement on health among those who retired for non-health reasons (Ekerdt, Bosse, & LoCastro, 1983).

Activity. There were few substantial effects of retirement on activities except for modest increases in solitary activities, self-care activities, time with friends, nonemployment work, and church attendance (DSLS data). The larger national study that had extensive data on activities (RHS) showed a notable lack of any substantial or significant effects of retirement. It appears that, except for the obvious reduction in time spent on the job and some compensating increase in solitary activities, retirement does not usually change men's patterns of social activities much or at all. Initial levels of activity were usually the strongest predictor of postretirement activity.

Attitudes. Retirement also had little or no effect on most attitude measures. Those few that showed significant effects were often inconsistent within or between studies. When such a large number of possible attitude effects are tested (we tested 56 possible effects), one can expect a few results (about 3) to be statistically significant at the .05 level by chance alone. There is certainly no clear evidence in these studies that retirement tends to make people depressed or dissatisfied with life.

Parnes (1981) reported that NLS retirees tend to be less satisfied with most aspects of life than nonretirees, but he did not control for initial differences. He found that healthy retirees were just as satisfied as nonretirees.

Early Retirement. All relevant analyses supported the conclusion that early retirement had stronger effects than retirement at or beyond age 65. A larger proportion of early retirees may have felt they had to retire because of poor health or lack of job opportunities, despite a greater loss of income. This hypothesis has been tested by analyzing the predictors and consequences of voluntary versus involuntary retirement (Chapter 6).

Several studies have found that early retirees are more likely to retire because of poor health (Parnes, 1981; Program Analysis Staff, 1982; Schwab, 1976) and have higher mortality rates than expected. Myers (1954), in a study of Civil Service employees retiring before compulsory retirement age, found those retiring before age 66 to have 9% to 21% higher than expected mortality rates. Haynes et al. (1978) found that rubber tire workers who retired before age 65 had substantially higher mortality rates than would be expected in a similar working group. The Social Security Administration (Program Analysis Staff, 1982) reports that insured workers claiming retirement benefits at age 62 have substantially higher mortality rates than others. All these studies support the hypothesis that the higher proportions of involuntary retirement (especially for poor health) among early retirees explains the stronger effects of early retirement compared with normal-age retirement.

No large or consistent differences were found in the effects of different measures of retirement. To put it another way, the small effects we found were similar regardless of which measure was used.

In conclusion, these analyses show that (1) when preretirement characteristics are controlled, most of the supposed negative consequences of retirement are small or insignificant, but (2) early retirement has more effect than later retirement. The evidence tends to support the hypotheses that retirement has different effects depending on type of outcome and timing of retirement.

5
Determinants of Adjustment

The purpose of this chapter is to examine the factors that affect adjustment among retirees and workers. At first glance, the topic of this chapter sounds much like that of the earlier chapter on the consequences of retirement. Yet this chapter is importantly different from the previous one in that the emphasis is upon the determinants of adjustment among retirees and among workers. The chapter on the consequences of retirement focused upon the degree to which having retired versus continuing to work affected multiple indicators of personal well-being. In general, the results, which included an examination of many consequences across multiple data sets, suggested that retirement *per se* had only limited effects upon the outcomes of interest. In this chapter, we examine the degree to which the same variables that predict good adjustment for retirees also predict good adjustment for those who remain in the labor force. This is a subtle difference—but an important one—and its implications will become clearer as we describe the way that this question was addressed and examine the results.

BACKGROUND AND RATIONALE

For the purposes of this chapter, adjustment will be defined as the level of subjective well-being reported by the respondent. Measures of happiness, life satisfaction, and related constructs will be the dependent variables examined. Individuals who describe themselves as satisfied or happy with their lives will be considered well adjusted; reports of unhappiness or dissatisfaction will be interpreted as indicators of poor adjustment. Admittedly, we have restricted the range of possible outcomes that could have been examined. For example, we could have determined whether the same variables that predict levels of self-rated health among the retired also predict levels of self-rated health among those who remain in the labor force. The purpose of this chapter, however, is to compare the determinants of overall life quality for retirees and nonretirees. Given that purpose, subjective well-being is the best single indicator of general life quality (George, 1980; George & Bearon, 1980). Moreover, as noted below, this definition of adjustment is compatible with previous research and, thus, this approach will maximize comparisons with previous studies.

A considerable body of literature addresses the general topic of adjustment during retirement. Many of these studies were restricted to retirees (rather than comparing retirees and nonretirees), and nearly all of them were based on cross-sectional data. In one of the earliest studies of adjustment during retirement, Simpson, Back, and McKinney (1966a, 1966b, 1966c, 1966d) examined the correlates of morale in a sample of retired men. The major factors found to correlate significantly with level of morale during retirement were occupational status, perceptions of job deprivation, orientation to retirement, amount of exposure to information about retirement, and the degree to which retirement activities were a direct and continuous extension of pre-retirement interests and activities. These findings are based on cross-sectional data. Adjustment during retirement was not predicted on the basis of preretirement status; nor were retirees compared to nonretirees. Thus, we do not know whether or not the results indicate patterns unique to adjustment during retirement.

Similarly, Atchley and his colleagues (Atchley, 1971b; Cottrell & Atchley, 1969) studied the adjustment of retired teachers and telephone company employees. A number of correlates of life satisfaction during retirement were identified. These correlates included work orientation, level of activity, self-rated health, and the ability to drive a car (a factor which facilitated the ability to engage in preferred social activities). Again, however, the results were based on a sample of retirees from whom data were obtained at one point in time. Many of the correlates of adjustment during retirement reported by Atchley also have been demonstrated to predict levels of subjective well-being among the older population in general (cf. Larson, 1978, for a review of the correlates of subjective well-being during later life). Thus, these vari-

ables may not be unique predictors of adjustment during retirement.

Longitudinal data and a sample that includes both retirees
and nonretirees does not ensure information about the predictors
of adjustment during retirement—although such design characteristics are essential to an adequate examination of the topic.
Streib and Schneider's classic study (1971), for example, included
both retirees and nonretirees, who were interviewed on multiple
occasions. Also, Streib and Schneider compared levels of life
satisfaction in the two groups over time, concluding that retirees
did not experience a significant decline in perceived quality of
life—compared both to their preretirement levels and to the
changes over time experienced by nonretirees. Similar findings
were reported by George and Maddox (1977), based upon a longitudinal study of male retirees and nonretirees. And, indeed, this
same general pattern of findings is true for the multiple samples
examined in this project, as described in the chapter on the consequences of retirement.

What no previous study has done, however, is to compare the
determinants of life quality for retirees and nonretirees using longitudinal data in a multivariate framework. Even though retirees
and older workers exhibit similar levels of subjective well-being,
the factors that produce perceptions of life quality may differ
across the two groups. Similarly, even if one's level of adjustment
remains stable throughout the retirement transition, different
variables may account for preretirement and postretirement adjustment—or the relative weights of the determinants of subjective
well-being may change during the transition. Thus, this chapter
compares the determinants of subjective well-being for retirees
with those of older workers. In addition to addressing a new research question, this chapter shares the same methodological ad-
vantages characteristic of other chapters in this volume: longitudinal data bases, use of a multivariate model, and replication
across multiple samples and diverse instrumentation. The replica-
tive nature of the analyses will permit us to assess the robustness
of the findings.

Analytic Strategy

Much of the current research that examines the determinants of
subjective well-being during later life relies upon path analysis

as a technique for hypothesizing a causal model and testing the compatibility of the model with the correlations observed in a particular data base (cf. Elwell & Maltbie-Crannell, 1981; Liang & Warfel, 1982; Mutran & Reitzes, 1981). Path analysis is not used in this chapter because we are not interested in unraveling the interrelationships among the independent variables that are hypothesized to affect levels of subjective well-being. A related analytic technique—hierarchical multiple regression—is employed, however, and an explicit model that arrays the independent variables along a series of stages of increasingly causal proximity to the dependent variable is tested.

The model that guides our analyses is comprised of four generic classes of independent variables: demographic variables, socioeconomic status, health, and activities and social relationships (see Figure 5.1). The classes of independent variables are added to the regression equations predicting subjective well-being one at a time, in the order presented above. This hierarchical order of entry permits us to observe the changing relationships between the independent variables and levels of subjective well-being as increasingly proximate predictors are added to the regression equations. In terms of predicting the dependent variable, hierarchical regression analysis provides as much information as path analysis (although the interrelationships among independent variables are not explored in depth). Thus, our basic model is one in which demographic variables are viewed as the least proximate predictors of subjective well-being. Socioeconomic status is viewed as the next most proximate predictor, followed by health. Finally, social activities and relationships are viewed as the most proximate predictors of subjective well-being. The stages in our hierarchical regression model are compatible with recent path models (cf. George & Landerman, in press; Herzog, Rodgers, & Woodworth, 1982).

The same model will be tested separately for persons who became retired during the course of the longitudinal studies and for those persons who continued to work throughout the entire survey period. This comparison will permit us to determine (1) whether the model predicts levels of subjective well-being equally well for the two groups, (2) whether those variables that are significant predictors of subjective well-being for the respondents who retired also are significant predictors of adjustment for respondents who remained in the labor force, and (3) whether the predictors that are significant for both groups are similar in magni-

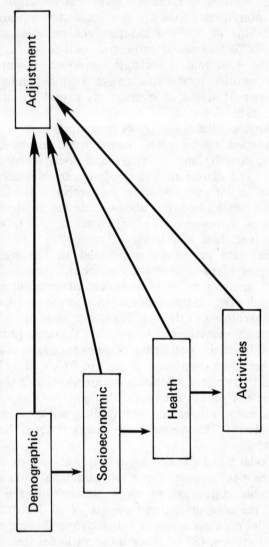

FIGURE 5.1. Theoretical model of predictors of adjustment for retirees and workers.

tude and direction of effect. The first comparison—overall model fit—will be assessed by a comparison of explained variance across the retirees and nonretirees. The second comparison—degree of similarity in predictors—will be determined by examination of the statistically significant predictors across the two groups. The final comparison—degree of similarity in the size and direction of individual predictors—will be assessed by examining unstandardized regression coefficients across the two groups.

In order to compare the determinants of adjustment of those who retire with that of those who continue to work, the measures of subjective well-being will, of necessity, be measured at the last test date. The most appropriate time of measurement for the independent variables, however, is less clear. On the one hand, subjective well-being would be expected to be most closely related to the individual's current social and personal situation. For example, current income, health, and level of activity should better predict current subjective well-being than previous economic status, health, and activity level. Further, retirement may directly affect some of the hypothesized determinants of subjective well-being (e.g., income)—and those effects which would differentiate retirees from nonretirees may be missed if preretirement variables are used to predict postretirement adjustment. For all of these reasons, a compelling case can be made for measuring the independent variables concurrently with the dependent variable at the last time of measurement.

On the other hand, it would be very useful if preretirement information could, in fact, be used to successfully predict adjustment during retirement. For example, the identification of key preretirement factors would greatly enhance the possibility of intervention designed to prevent poor adjustment during retirement. Putting this possibility to empirical test would require predicting subjective well-being at a later point in time (when some of the respondents were retired) on the basis of independent variables measured previously (when all of the respondents were working).

Thus, there are important reasons for predicting the adjustment of those who retire and those who continue to work both concurrently and prospectively. Both types of analyses are reported in this chapter. In the prospective applications, independent variables measured at the first test date (when all respondents were working) are used to predict levels of subjective well-being at the last test date (at which point some respondents have retired and others continue to work). In the concurrent applications, both the independent variables and the dependent variable are measured at the last test date.

METHODS

Data Sources

Only two of the data sets used in this project included sufficient numbers of retirees and nonretirees to permit meaningful analyses of the determinants of subjective well-being: the National Longitudinal Survey of Older Men (NLS) and the Retirement History Study (RHS).

As described previously, the NLS is an ongoing longitudinal study of the labor force participation of mature men. For the analyses reported in this chapter, baseline measures were obtained in 1966 and the last test date was 1976. Initially, the NLS included a nationally representative sample of 5020 men aged 45 to 59. Blacks were oversampled by a factor of about three to one. In order to be included in the analyses reported in this chapter, respondents had to meet three criteria: (1) present in both the 1966 (baseline) and 1976 (outcome) test dates, (2) have been employed at least 16 hours a week in 1966, and (3) have not been retired in 1966. (Retirement was defined using our definition of objective retirement, described in detail in Chapter 2.) These selection criteria were used in order to restrict the sample to those respondents for whom longitudinal data were available and to compare those who retired during the study with those who remained in the labor force. Application of the selection criteria resulted in a sample of 1985 respondents: 657 who remained in the labor force and 1328 who retired.

The RHS began with a nationally representative sample of 11,153 men and unmarried women aged 58 to 63. For the analyses reported in this chapter, the baseline data were obtained in 1969 and the outcome data were measured in 1975. To reduce computer costs, the analyses were performed on a one-third random subsample of RHS participants. Use of the one-third sampling strategy and application of the selection criteria resulted in a sample of 1824 respondents: 462 who worked throughout the survey and 1362 who retired during the study.

Measures

We attempted to extract five classes of variables from each survey: the four classes of independent variables described previously and indicators of subjective well-being. The measures used in this chapter are described briefly below; detailed descriptions of the measures are provided in the Appendix.

Demographic Variables. With one exception, identical demographic variables were extracted from the two data sets. Age was measured in years. Marital status was measured as a dichotomous variable, with 0 indicating unmarried and 1 representing being married. Education was measured as years of formal schooling. Race was a dichotomous variable with 0 representing white respondents and 1 representing black respondents. For both data sets, the few respondents who reported another racial identity were omitted from analysis. All NLS participants were male, but gender is included in the RHS analyses. Sex was coded as a dichotomous variable, with 0 representing men and 1 representing women.

Socioeconomic Status. Because education was included among the demographic indicators, this class of variables consists of measures of economic status. The NLS included two relevant measures: family income and family assets. Both were measured in dollar amounts. The income measure used from the RHS is a measure of income adequacy. This measure was developed by adjusting household income by the number of dependents, scaling the metric to the Intermediate Budget of the U.S. Department of Labor. Higher scale scores represent increased economic adequacy.

Health. In both the NLS and RHS, health is measured such that higher scores represent increased health limitations or impairments. The NLS measure is a single-item indicator and the RHS measure is a scale based on responses to four items.

Activities and Social Relationships. Unfortunately, the NLS did not include measures of participation in formal and informal social activities and relationships. Consequently, analyses of the NLS data are restricted to three-stage hierarchical regression equations. Because activity and social relationship variables are hypothesized to be the most proximate predictors of subjective well-being, we anticipate that the total proportions of explained variance will be lower in the NLS than in the RHS analyses.

In contrast, the RHS included several measures of activities and social relationships. Multi-item scales were used to measure participation in formal organizations, time spent in extra-work interests (including home maintenance and other instrumental activities), interactions with family, interaction with friends, and time spent in solitary activities.

Subjective Well-Being. The NLS included a single-item measure of life satisfaction. Respondents reported their overall satisfaction with life along a four-point continuum ranging from very dissatisfied to very satisfied. The RHS included a four-item scale that also tapped global life satisfaction. Higher scores represent increased satisfaction on both measures.

RESULTS

Findings from the NLS

Tables 5.1 and 5.2 present the hierarchical regression equations predicting life satisfaction for nonretirees and retirees in the NLS. Table 5.1 provides the prospective models; Table 5.2 presents the concurrent models. For each set of equations, both unstandardized (b's) and standardized (B's) regression coefficients are presented. The former are used to compare coefficients across the two groups; the standardized regression coefficients are useful for examining the relative strength of predictors within groups. As noted earlier, discussion of findings will focus upon three types of comparisons across retirees and nonretirees: (1) overall model fit, (2) similarity of predictors, and (3) effect sizes of predictors.

For the prospective models (Table 5.1), the overall fit of the model, in terms of explained variance, is poor for both groups. The total R^2 for nonretirees is 1%; for retirees, 4%. The amount of explained variance is larger for retirees than for nonretirees— and, in fact, achieves statistical significance. Nonetheless, the total proportion of explained variance for retirees is very low. None of the independent variables included in the model is a significant predictor of life satisfaction for nonretirees. Three predictors are significant predictors of subjective well-being among the retirees: age (the older the respondent, the greater the life satisfaction), family income (higher income predicts higher life satisfaction), and health limitations (the higher the health limitations, the lower the life satisfaction). Education is positively related to the life satisfaction of retirees net of other demographic variables,

TABLE 5.1
Regression Equations Predicting Life Satisfaction, NLS, Prospective Models

	Nonretirees						Retirees					
	Stage 1		Stage 2		Stage 3		Stage 1		Stage 2		Stage 3	
Independent Variables	b	B	b	B	b	B	b	B	b	B	b	B
Age	.00	.01	.00	.00	.00	.00	.02[a]	.07[a]	.02[a]	.06[a]	.02[a]	.06[a]
Marital status	.07	.04	.06	.03	.06	.03	.10	.04	.06	.03	.06	.03
Education	.01	.07	.01	.03	.01	.03	.02[b]	.11[b]	.01	.07	.01	.06
Race	.04	.03	.05	.04	.05	.04	.02	.01	.04	.02	.02	.01
Family income			.00	.08	.00	.08			.00[a]	.10[a]	.00	.08[a]
Assets			.00	.05	.00	.05			.00	.04	.00	.04
Health limitations					-.05	-.03					-.16[b]	-.10[b]
R^2		.01		.01		.01		.02[a]		.03[a]		.04[a]

[a] $p \leq .05$
[b] $p \leq .01$

TABLE 5.2
Regression Equations Predicting Life Satisfaction, NLS, Concurrent Models

Independent Variables	Nonretirees						Retirees					
	Stage 1		Stage 2		Stage 3		Stage 1		Stage 2		Stage 3	
	b	B	b	B	b	B	b	B	b	B	b	B
Age	.01	.02	.00	.02	.00	.01	.02[a]	.07[a]	.02[a]	.07[a]	.02[a]	.07[a]
Marital status	.27[b]	.16[b]	.26[b]	.16[b]	.27[b]	.16[b]	.23[b]	.12[b]	.21[b]	.11[b]	.21[b]	.11[b]
Education	.01	.06	.01	.04	.01	.04	.02[b]	.11[b]	.02[a]	.08[a]	.01	.04
Race	.05	.04	.06	.04	.06	.04	.03	.02	.05	.03	.06	.04
Family income			.00	.04	.00	.02			.00	.05	.00	.04
Assets			.00	.04	.00	.04			.00	.06	.00	.06
Health limitations					-.20[b]	-.14[b]					-.33[b]	-.23[b]
R^2	.03[a]		.03		.05[a]		.03[a]		.09[b]		.09[b]	

[a] $p \leqslant .05$
[b] $p \leqslant .01$

but this relationship is reduced to nonsignificance once the indicators of socioeconomic status are added to the model. As would be expected on the basis of the tests of statistical significance, the unstandardized regression coefficients for age and health limitations are higher for the retirees than for the nonretirees. Interestingly, however, the *b*'s for family income are identical in the two groups—and yet the effects of income are significant for the retirees, but not the nonretirees. This pattern reflects the fact that tests of statistical significance are highly affected by sample size—because the group of retirees is much larger than the group of nonretirees, smaller coefficients will attain statistical significance for the former.

Table 5.2, which presents the concurrent models for NLS retirees and nonretirees, exhibits some of the same patterns as those observed in Table 5.1. The model fits the data for retirees slightly better than those for nonretirees (total R^2 = 9% and 5%, respectively). Health limitations and age are again significant predictors of life satisfaction for the retirees. The concurrent analyses also differ from the prospective ones in important ways, however. First, for both groups, the concurrent models explain more total variance in levels of subjective well-being than the prospective analyses. As noted earlier, this undoubtedly reflects the fact that current well-being is more closely related to current social and personal status. Second, two significant predictors of life satisfaction emerged for the nonretirees: marital status and health limitations. As would be expected, being married and lower levels of health limitations are related to higher life satisfaction. Third, the concurrent predictors of subjective well-being for retirees differ from both the concurrent predictors for nonretirees and the prospective predictors for retirees. As was true for nonretirees, marital status and health limitations are significant concurrent predictors of retirees' levels of life satisfaction. One additional variable, age, was significant for retirees but not for nonretirees. Comparing the prospective and concurrent analyses for the retirees, we see that although health and age are significant predictors in both models, each time of measurement also has a unique significant predictor. Thus, family income predicts retirees' levels of life satisfaction in the prospective, but not the concurrent, model. Conversely, marital status is a significant predictor of retirees' subjective well-being in the concurrent but not the prospective, model.

When examining the overall fit of the NLS models, two notes of caution are prudent. First, as noted previously, the low proportions of explained variance undoubtedly reflect, in part, the fact that the NLS included no indicators of social activities—the generic class of independent variables hypothesized to be the most proximate predictors of subjective well-being. A second factor that probably contributes to the poor overall fit of the models is the nature of the dependent variable. Use of a nonstandardized, single-item indicator of subjective well-being (such as that available in the NLS) typically results in lower estimates than use of standardized, multi-item scales (cf. George, 1981; George & Landerman, in press).

Findings from the RHS

Table 5.3 presents the prospective equations predicting the life satisfaction of retirees and nonretirees in the RHS. In terms of overall model fit, the R^2 values are nearly identical for the two groups (R^2 = .23 for nonretirees, R^2 = .22 for retirees). Thus the model predicts subjective well-being equally well for both groups. Four of the independent variables are significant predictors of subjective well-being for both groups: education, income inadequacy, health limitations, and time spent in solitary activities. In addition to being significant predictors for both groups, the four independent variables exhibited approximately equal magnitudes and were in the same direction. Thus, higher levels of educational attainment, higher levels of income adequacy, lower levels of health limitations, and increased time pursuing solitary leisure activities were associated, net of other predictors, with higher levels of life satisfaction. There also were unique predictors of subjective well-being for each of the groups. For nonretirees, race, marital status, and amount of interaction with friends were significant independent variables. Being black lowered life satisfaction scores, being married and increased amounts of interaction with friends increased life satisfaction scores (although the effects of interaction with friends was quite weak). For retirees (but not for nonretirees), increased participation in formal organizations was related to increased life satisfaction.

Table 5.4 presents the concurrent analyses for the nonretirees and retirees in the RHS. Both groups exhibited relatively high proportions of explained variance—31% for the nonretirees and 35% for the retirees. As was true for the prospective analyses, the models fit the two groups equally well. Compatible with the NLS

TABLE 5.3
Regression Equations Predicting Life Satisfaction, RHS, Prospective Models

Independent Variables	Nonretirees								Retirees							
	Stage 1		Stage 2		Stage 3		Stage 4		Stage 1		Stage 2		Stage 3		Stage 4	
	b	B	b	B	b	B	b	B	b	B	b	B	b	B	b	B
Age	.06	.05	.07	.06	.06	.05	.07	.05	-.01	-.01	-.01[b]	-.01[b]	-.03	-.02	-.03	.02
Marital status	.44	.10	.59[a]	.13[a]	.59[a]	.13[a]	.57[a]	.13[a]	.52[a]	.11[a]	.57[a]	.12[a]	.53[a]	.12[a]	.22	.05
Education	.12[b]	.23[b]	.08[b]	.16[b]	.08[a]	.15[a]	.06[a]	.12[a]	.19[b]	.31[b]	.14[b]	.23[b]	.13[b]	.22[b]	.07[a]	.12[a]
Race	-1.64[b]	-.25[b]	-1.41[b]	-.22[b]	-1.44[b]	-.22[b]	-1.39[b]	-.22[b]	-.53[a]	-.07[a]	-.29	-.04	-.32	-.04	-.24	-.03
Sex	.17	.04	.35	.07	.34	.07	.22	.04	.06	.01	.17	.03	.11	.02	.39	.01
Income adequacy			.23[b]	.17[b]	.21[b]	.16[b]	.18[a]	.14[a]			.33[b]	.23[b]	.31[b]	.22[b]	.23[b]	.17[b]
Health limitations					-.12[b]	-.15[b]	-.11[a]	-.13[a]					-.09[a]	-.13[a]	-.09[b]	-.17[b]
Formal organizations							.00	.01							.04[b]	.18[b]
Extra-work interests							-.03	-.05							.04	.05
Family contact							.01	.04							-.01	-.03
Friend contact							.07[a]	.12[a]							.03	.05
Solitary activities							.19[a]	.14[a]							.11[a]	.07[a]
R^2	.15[a]		.17[a]		.19[b]		.23[b]		.12[a]		.16[a]		.18[b]		.22[b]	

[a] $p \leq .05$
[b] $p \leq .01$

63

TABLE 5.4
Regression Equations Predicting Life Satisfaction, RHS, Concurrent Models

	Nonretirees								Retirees							
	Stage 1		Stage 2		Stage 3		Stage 4		Stage 1		Stage 2		Stage 3		Stage 4	
Independent Variables	b	B	b	B	b	B	b	B	b	B	b	B	b	B	b	B
Age	.06	.05	.08	.06	.06	.05	.06	.05	-.01	-.01	.00	.00	.00	.00	.00	.00
Marital status	.44	.10	.69a	.16a	.65a	.15a	.55a	.12a	.52a	.11a	.49a	.11a	.42a	.09a	.13	.03
Education	.12b	.23b	.05a	.10a	.05a	.09a	.02	.03	.19b	.31b	.08a	.13a	.07a	.11a	.03	.05
Race	-1.64b	-.25b	-.98b	-.15b	-.94b	-.15b	-.89b	-.14b	-.53a	-.07a	-.35	-.05	-.39a	-.05a	-.32	-.04
Sex	.17	.04	.41	.08	.39	.08	.31	.06	.06	.01	.18	.04	.09	.02	-.06	-.01
Income adequacy			.49b	.37b	.45b	.34b	.39b	.30b			.64b	.44b	.58b	.40b	.49b	.34b
Health limitations					-.08a	-.12a	-.06a	-.09a					-.13b	-.23b	-.12b	-.21b
Formal organizations							.02	.09							.04b	.14b
Extra-work interests							.02	.03							.04a	.05a
Family contact							-.00	-.04							.00	.01
Friend contact							.07a	.13a							.03a	.06a
Solitary activities							.13a	.09a							.08a	.05a
R^2	.15a		.26b		.27b		.31b		.12a		.28b		.33b		.35b	

[a] $p \le .05$
[b] $p \le .01$

64

findings, the concurrent models exhibited better fit for both groups than did the prospective models. Four of the independent variables were significant predictors of subjective well-being for both retirees and nonretirees. Life satisfaction for both groups is positively related to income adequacy, fewer health limitations, increased interaction with friends, and increased time in solitary leisure activities. Again, however, some independent variables emerged as significant predictors for only one group. For non-retirees, being black was associated with decreased levels of subjective well-being and being married was associated with greater life satisfaction. Interestingly, for retirees both of these variables remained significant predictors through the third stage of analysis, but were reduced to nonsignificance after the social activity measures entered the equation. Participation in formal organizations and time spent in extra-work interests were unique predictors of retirees' life satisfaction. As might be expected, both measures were positively related to level of subjective well-being.

DISCUSSION

The purpose of this chapter was to determine whether the determinants of subjective well-being are the same for retirees and nonretirees. This issue was examined by applying a theoretical model to two data sets using hierarchical multiple regression. In each data set the determinants of subjective well-being were examined separately for retirees and nonretirees, and both prospective and concurrent analyses were generated. The models of adjustment for retirees and nonretirees were compared in terms of overall fit (i.e., amount of explained variance) and the effects of specific independent variables. To our knowledge, this is the first study to compare the determinants of well-being among retirees and nonretirees using longitudinal data and a multivariate model.

The results are mixed with regard to the degree to which the same factors that account for good adjustment among older workers also predict successful adjustment among retirees. Overall, the theoretical model predicted levels of subjective well-being equally well for both groups. Moreover, within data sets, a common group of independent variables typically were significant predictors of adjustment for both retirees and nonretirees—and, for those variables, the directions and magnitudes of the regression coefficients were similar across the two groups. These findings support the contention that the same set of determinants account for the adjustment of both retirees and nonretirees. And yet the results are equivocal because group-specific predictors also were identified—and those unique predictors usually made sound theoretical sense. For example, in the RHS data, social activities were more frequently significant predictors of life satisfaction for retirees than for nonretirees. This pattern may indicate that retirees use various social activities as substitutes for work and, thus, amount of participation in such activities predicts subjective well-being for retirees, but not for older workers. Thus, although the majority of evidence suggests that the same set of independent variables predicts adjustment for both retirees and nonretirees, there also appear to be a limited number of predictors that have differential effects depending upon the employment status of the respondents.

Within data sets, separate analyses also were generated to compare prospective and concurrent models of adjustment. The prospective models included baseline independent variables (at which point all the respondents were working) and subjective well-being measures from a later point in time (when some respondents had retired and others remained in the labor force). In the concurrent models, both the independent and dependent variables were measured at the final test date. As expected, concurrent models generated greater proportions of explained variance than the prospective models, reflecting the fact that subjective well-being is most closely related to individuals' current characteristics and situations. Yet the prospective models were not greatly different from the concurrent ones. That is, although the concurrent models generated better fit in absolute terms, in relative terms the differences were small. This suggests that the determinants of subjective well-being for both retirees and nonretirees are relatively stable over time.

The primary justification for the prospective models was the possibility of identifying antecedents of poor adjustment in retirement that are amenable to intervention. In this regard the results are not encouraging. First, almost none of the significant predictors identified in the prospective analyses are easily manipulated by public programs. Second, there were few significant predictors that emerged during the prospective analyses that applied only to the retirees. Most of the significant predictors identified in the prospective analyses are general resources or characteristics that affect both retirees and nonretirees. Thus, those predictors are not sensitive variables for identifying respondents at risk of poor adjustment during retirement. On the other hand, as described in earlier chapters, few of the respondents exhibited evidence of poor adjustment to retirement. Thus, the scope of this policy-relevant issue may be limited.

The results reported in this chapter should not be viewed as the final word on the determinants of adjustment for retirees and nonretirees. Indeed, it would be appropriate to view these findings as initial explorations on an important topic. Fruitful areas for further research include replication with other data sets, especially data sets that are richer in sociological and psychological content than the surveys available for analysis in this chapter, and comparisons of path models across groups of retirees and nonretirees. The major contribution of this chapter has been the demonstration that this is an important and neglected topic that holds promise of generating useful findings.

6
Reasons for Retirement

There has been considerable interest and research on reasons for retirement (Morgan, 1980; Motley, 1978; Palmore, 1971; Parnes, 1981; Streib & Schneider, 1971). This research has dealt with the theoretical question of why people retire as well as the more policy-oriented questions of what difference the reasons for retirement make in the effects of retirement. Our interpretations of the findings on predictors and consequences of retirement were based on various assumptions about reasons for retirement.

Most of the previous research on reasons for retirement have used either cross-sectional data or only bivariate analyses. This chapter uses longitudinal multivariate analyses to analyze the predictors and consequences of reasons for retirement. We are particularly concerned with those who have to retire involuntarily. Are they a disadvantaged group before retirement and do they suffer negative effects of retirement more than those who retire voluntarily?

Previous research has indicated that involuntary retirees are both disadvantaged before, and suffer more after, retirement. For example, an analysis of 1486 recent retirees found that the involuntary retirees tended to have lower income, lower occupation, and poorer health before retirement (Kimmel, Price, & Walker, 1978). However, these findings were based on retrospective data and so may be biased. They also found that the involuntary retirees had lower income, poorer health, less retirement satisfaction, but more employment after retirement. Similarly, a smaller study of 140 retired men found that involuntary retirees had significantly lower emotional satisfaction and feelings of usefulness, poorer self-images, less emotional stability, and fewer interpersonal relations (Peretti & Wilson, 1975).

TYPES OF REASONS

Three of the longitudinal surveys contained data on reasons for retirement (NLS, RHS, and DSLS). We focused on those data which allowed us to categorize retirees as voluntary or involuntary. At first we tried analyses using the dichotomy of voluntary or involuntary, but it became apparent that the involuntary category included two rather different groups: those who had to retire because of health limitations and those who had to retire for other involuntary reasons, such as mandatory retirement at a certain age or being laid off. Therefore, most of our analyses were based on a trichotomy of reasons: voluntary, health limitation, and other compulsory reasons.

In the RHS analysis there was one ambiguous response category: retiring because of "age." Since we could not determine whether these were voluntary retirements (wanting to retire because they were old) or involuntary (having to retire because of reaching a certain age), we decided to exclude them from the final analyses.

Table 6.1 presents the percentage distributions of those retiring for health, other compulsory, or voluntary reasons for the NLS, RHS, and DSLS. In the NLS a little over one-third retired for health reasons, one-quarter for other compulsory reasons, and a little over one-third for voluntary reasons. In the RHS also a little over one-third retired for health reasons, but fewer (16%) said they retired for compulsory reasons and more (50%) said they retired for voluntary reasons. We believe this discrepancy is accounted for by the omission of those who gave "age" as the rea-

TABLE 6.1
Reasons for Retirement[a]

Study	N	Percentage Distribution by Reason		
		Health	Compulsory	Voluntary
NLS	860	39	25	36
RHS[b]	655	34	16	50
DSLS	85	11	41	48

[a]*NLS and RHS retirees are men only. DSLS includes men and women.*

[b]*RHS retirees who gave "age" as reason were omitted from analysis.*

sons for retirement: we think most of these would have been compulsory reasons; e.g., mandatory retirement based on age. In the DSLS by contrast, only one-tenth said they had to retire because of health. This indicates that this sample was a relatively healthy group of retirees.

Thus, depending on the sample and the method of asking for reasons, about one-third to one-half said they retired voluntarily and about one-half to two thirds retired for health or other compulsory reasons. It is clear that involuntary retirement is a widespread problem, affecting the majority of retirees. But in addition to distinguishing between the voluntary and involuntary retired, we want to further distinguish between those who had to retire because of poor health and those who had to retire for other compulsory reasons.

PREDICTORS OF REASONS
FOR RETIREMENT

Who are the involuntary retirees? How are they different from the voluntary retirees? We used canonical correlation analysis with voluntary reasons as the omitted category to answer this question (Tables 6.2-6.4). The NLS, with the most cases, showed the most significant predictors and had two significant canonical variates (Table 6.2). The first canonical variate shows that those who retired for health reasons were quite different from those who retired for other compulsory or for voluntary reasons, and the latter two categories were quite similar to each other. The strongest predictor of retirement because of health, as might be expected, was having health-related work limitations before retirement. In addition, it shows that low socioeconomic status (occupation and education) is also strongly predictive of retiring for health reasons (rather than for other compulsory or voluntary reasons). It also shows that younger age predicts retirement for health reasons. This fits with our other findings which show poor health to be a stronger predictor of early retirement than later retirement.

The second canonical variate in the NLS distinguishes between those who retired for compulsory reasons versus voluntary reasons. This shows the strongest predictor of retiring for compulsory reasons to be older age (because compulsory retirement based on age affects more older workers). Also being employed by others (as opposed to being self-employed) strongly predicts

TABLE 6.2
Predictors of Reasons for Retirement among NLS Men[a]

	Canonical Variate 1	Canonical Variate 2
Predictors		
Demographic		
Age	-.20	.57
Rural	.02	-.09
Health		
Work limitations	.53	.28
Socioeconomic		
Wage	-.11	-.08
Poverty ratio	-.01	-.02
Occupation	-.25	-.15
Education	-.24	.30
Job characteristics		
Hours per year	-.13	-.10
Mandatory retirement	-.09	.28
Pension	-.13	-.31
Self-employed	.20	-.41
Number of employees	.06	.19
Attitudes		
Pro-job	-.14	.36
Pro-retirement	-.05	-.12
Work more important than wages	-.03	-.41
Reasons for Retirement		
Health	1.01	.49
Compulsory	.03	1.12
Voluntary	.00	.00
Canonical Correlation	.18[b]	.05[b]

[a]*N = 860. Ages 62–69 in 1976.*

[b]*Significant at .01 level.*

retirement for compulsory reasons (since only those employed by others are subject to mandatory retirement rules). Having pro-job attitudes also predicts compulsory retirement, which shows that those who like their jobs tend to keep working until they are forced to retire. Finally, and somewhat surprisingly, those who said that what they most liked about their job was the work rather than the wages were more likely to retire voluntarily. Perhaps this is because those who said the wages are more important had to keep working for the income until compulsory retirement age.

The analysis of the RHS predictors of reasons for retirement was useful mainly to distinguish between those retiring for health versus those retiring voluntarily (since those giving "age" as a reason were omitted, most of whom probably would have been retired for compulsory reasons). The canonical correlations show that the strongest predictors of retiring for health reasons were the same as in the NLS: poor health, lower socioeconomic status, and younger age (Table 6.3). In addition, it shows that those with lower life satisfaction and without pensions are more likely to retire for health reasons.

The analysis of the DSLS predictors was useful in distinguishing between those retiring for compulsory reasons versus health reasons (voluntary retirees fell in between those two types). The strongest predictors of retiring for health reasons were again younger age and lower education (Table 6.4). In addition, those with high negative affect were more likely to retire for poor health, which is similar to the RHS finding of lower life satisfaction as a predictor of retirement for poor health. In contrast, those with high anomie were more likely to retire for compulsory reasons.

TABLE 6.3
Predictors of Reasons for Retirement among RHS Men[a]

	Canonical Variate
Predictors	
Age	-.33
Health	.52
Education	.05
Socioeconomic factor	.35
Pension	.25
Solitary/sedentary activities	.08
Life satisfaction	.29
Reasons for Retirement	
Health	-.99
Compulsory	-.67
Voluntary	.00
Canonical Correlation	.27[b]

[a]*N = 655. Ages 64–69 in 1976.*
[b]*Significant at .01 level.*

TABLE 6.4
Predictors of Reasons for Retirement among DSLS Men and Women[a]

	Canonical Variate
Predictors	
Age	.56
Sex	.23
Education	.53
Time spent in solitary activity	-.28
Anomie	.44
Future orientation	.21
Status dimension of self-concept	-.26
Negative affect	-.59
Reasons for Retirement	
Compulsory retirement	.76
Retirement due to poor health	-.46
Voluntary retirement (omitted category)	.00
Canonical Correlation	.56[b]

[a]*N = 85 (56 men and 29 women). Ages 56+ in 1974–76.*
[b]*Significant at .01 level.*

In summary, the predictors of reasons for retirement from these three studies are fairly consistent. Those retiring because of poor health were a relatively deprived group before retirement. They had more health related work limitations, had lower socio-economic status, and lower life satisfaction (or more negative affect). In contrast, those retiring for other compulsory reasons tended to be older, had higher socioeconomic status, were employed by others, and had pro-job attitudes. Thus, the compulsory retired and the voluntarily retired tended to be more advantaged than those retiring for poor health.

CONSEQUENCES OF INVOLUNTARY RETIREMENT

Does retirement tend to have more negative effects on those who retire for health or compulsory reasons than on those who retire voluntarily? In order to answer this question, we did a series of multiple regression analyses of retired persons, one for each theoretically possible consequence of retirement, in which all the significant Time 1 predictors (including the baseline measure of the consequence variable) were entered as independent variables in the first stage and the two involuntary reasons (health and compulsory) were entered as independent dummy variables in the second stage to see if they significantly increased the variance explained and, if so, the direction and strength of their effect. This is similar to the method used in the "Consequences" chapter, except the present analysis is restricted to the retired only.

The results were fairly consistent. First, those retiring for compulsory reasons were not substantially different from other retirees on *any* consequences except for one. In the DSLS, retiring for compulsory reasons decreased negative affect (Table 6.5). On the other hand, it had no significant effect on life satisfaction nor affect balance nor any other consequence in the DSLS. There were *no* significant effects of compulsory retirement in the RHS (Table 6.6) and all the effects in the NLS were negligible (R^2 increase of .01 or less, Table 6.7).

Second, retirement for health reasons had several negative consequences. Living standard was substantially reduced in the NLS by retirement for health. Health declined much more in all three studies, although much of this decline probably occurred between the first survey and retirement (see discussion in "Consequences" chapter). Age identification more often shifted to

TABLE 6.5
Significant Consequences of Retirement for Health or Compulsory Reasons among DSLS Men and Women[a]

Consequence	Total R^2 without Reason for Retirement	R^2 Increase due to Retirement for	
		Health	Compulsory Reasons
Health(−)	.36	.08	
Internal orientation(−)	.33	.06	
Age identification(+)	.36	.03	
Life satisfaction(−)	.35	.05	
Negative affect(−)	.23		.04

[a]*Analysis based on about 85 retired men and women aged 52-76 in 1976. Only consequences significant at .05 level and increasing variance explained by .005 or more are shown. Consequences tested but found not significant include income, church attendance, psychosomatic symptoms, all activity measures, future orientation, social value, usefulness, anomie, positive affect, and affect balance. Plus or minus signs indicate positive or negative associations.*

TABLE 6.6
Significant Consequences of Retirement for
Health or Compulsory Reasons among RHS Men[a]

Consequence	Total R^2 without Reason for Retirement	R^2 Increase due to Retirement for	
		Health	Compulsory Reasons
Income adequacy(-)	.34	.01	(none significant)
Health factor(-)	.16	.04	
Extra-work interests(-)	.52	.01	
Activity satisfaction(-)	.08	.01	
Life satisfaction(-)	.32	.01	
Retirement attitude(-)	.03	.02	

[a]*Analysis based on about 655 retired men aged 64–69 in 1975. Consequences tested but found not significant include income, worry about finances, socioeconomic factor, formal organizations, attitude to work, social-family, social-friends, and solitary-sedentary. Plus or minus signs indicate positive or negative associations.*

TABLE 6.7
Significant Consequences of Retirement for
Health or Compulsory Reasons among NLS Men[a]

Consequence	Total R^2 without Reason for Retirement	R^2 Increase due to Retirement for	
		Health	Compulsory Reasons
Assets(+)	.24		.01
Living standard(-)	.12	.04	.01
Health limits(+)	.19	.20	.01
Health factor(-)	.18	.15	.01
Health satisfaction(-)	.14	.12	.01
Leisure satisfaction(-)	.07	.04	.01
Life satisfaction(-)	.04	.04	.01

[a]*Analysis based on about 860 retired men aged 62–69 in 1976. Only consequences significant at .05 level and increasing variance explained by .005 or more are shown. Consequences tested but found not significant include income, poverty ratio, satisfaction with residence, and internal orientation. Plus or minus signs indicate positive or negative associations.*

75

older categories (DSLS). Finally, various measures of satisfaction (with life, leisure, activity, and retirement) declined significantly in all studies following retirement for health reasons.

In summary, our analyses consistently show that those retiring for poor health suffered significantly more negative effects from their retirement than other retirees, and that those retiring for other compulsory reasons did not experience substantially more negative effects than other retirees. It should be understood that these results were found after controlling for preretirement characteristics and so cannot be explained by initial disadvantage.

Why are the effects of retirement for poor health so much more negative than the effects of retirement for other compulsory reasons? There are probably several reasons. First, those who retire because of mandatory retirement based on age are more likely to have worked for large corporations with good pension systems. Their better pensions reduced the negative effects of earnings loss. Secondly, mandatory retirement is something that can be prepared for years in advance to prevent negative effects. Third, those retiring for mandatory rules were more likely to have the option of getting some part-time work, if desired, to supplement their income and give a greater sense of usefulness. Those retired for poor health tended to be disabled and not have the option of part-time work. Finally, saying that one retired because of poor health is an admission of disability and this may lower self-esteem, in contrast to those who had to retire because of mandatory retirement based on an arbitrary age. The latter group can maintain that they are just as capable as before retirement.

CONSEQUENCES OF INVOLUNTARY RETIREMENT FOR EARLY RETIREES

Because our earlier analyses showed that early retirees suffer more negative effects than "on-time" retirees, we repeated the above type of analysis for the early retirees only, those aged 62 to 64 and retired by the end of the study. We could do this only for NLS because the RHS did not have persons under age 64 at the end and the DSLS had too few cases in this category.

When we compare the effects of involuntary retirement among early retirees (Table 6.8) with those among all retirees (Table 6.7), we see that the negative effects are consistently greater among the early retirees, as measured by the R^2 increases. Furthermore,

TABLE 6.8
Significant Consequences of Early Retirement
for Health or Compulsory Reasons among NLS Men[a]

Consequence	Total R^2 without Reason for Retirement	R^2 Increase due to Retirement for	
		Health	Compulsory Reasons
Assets(−)	.24		.02
Living standard(−)	.13	.05	
Health limits(+)	.24	.21	.02
Health factor(−)	.19	.15	.02
Health satisfaction(−)	.16	.13	.02
Leisure satisfaction(−)	.07	.06	.02
Life satisfaction(−)	.10	.06	.01
Residence satisfaction(−)	.00		.02
Internal orientation(−)	.10		.02

[a]*Analysis based on about 295 retired men aged 62–64 in 1976. Consequences tested but found not significant include income and poverty ratio. Also see note to Table 6.5.*

retirement for other compulsory reasons had two significant negative effects among early retirees that were not significant among all retirees: lower residence satisfaction and internal orientation. However, all of these negative effects among early retirees were only slightly greater than among all retirees: the R^2 increases were only one or two points greater among the early retirees. Thus, the pattern of effects were similar and the size of the effects were only slightly greater among early retirees.

CONSEQUENCES OF VOLUNTARY RETIREMENT

These findings led to another question: does voluntary retirement have any positive effects? One might assume that most of those who retire voluntarily do so because they expect their retirement to have positive effects. We decided that the best way to answer this question was to compare those who voluntarily retired with those who continued to work in the same age cohort. We repeated the multiple regression analyses used for the "Consequences" chapter (which includes the retired and nonretired), but this time omitting those who retired for involuntary reasons (health or other compulsory), so that the final independent (dummy) variable was coded a 0 for the nonretired and a 1 for the voluntary retired.

Tables 6.9-6.11 show that when all voluntarily retired are compared to those not retired, there are little or no differences for most consequences, a few significant positive effects, but some income loss among those who voluntarily retire after age 64. Let us consider each type of possible consequence in more detail.

Finances. In the NLS, which includes men aged 62 to 69 at the end, there were no significant effects of voluntary retirement on income, assets, or the poverty ratio (Table 6.9). Satisfaction with living standard showed a positive effect of voluntary retirement (R^2 increase = .04). The RHS, which includes only men aged 64 to 69 at the end, shows a *loss* of income due to voluntary retirement (R^2 increase = .06, Table 6.10). However, voluntary retirement has a *positive* effect on income *adequacy*. Since income adequacy takes into account the number and types of dependents, this means that the loss of income was more than made up for by a decline in income needs. Apparently, many of the voluntary retirees are able to retire because they have fewer dependents than before and so their income is more adequate after retirement despite a drop in absolute amount. This is also reflected by the lack of effect on "worry about finances." The DSLS also shows a drop in absolute income, but has no measure of income adequacy.

Health. All three surveys agree that the voluntarily retired stay as healthy as those who continue working. There are no significant effects for any of the measures of health except one,

TABLE 6.9
Significant Consequences of Voluntary Retirement among NLS Men[a]

Consequence	Total R^2 without Voluntary Retirement	R^2 Increase for Voluntary Retirement
Living standard(+)	.10	.04
Leisure satisfaction(+)	.04	.01
Life satisfaction(+)	.07	.01

[a] *Analysis based on about 828 working or voluntarily retired men aged 62-69 in 1976. Consequences tested but found not significant include income, assets, poverty ratio, health limits, health factor, health satisfaction, and residence satisfaction. See also note to Table 6.5.*

TABLE 6.10
Significant Consequences of Voluntary Retirement among RHS Men[a]

Consequence	Total R^2 without Voluntary Retirement	R^2 Increase for Voluntary Retirement
Income(−)	.13	.06
Income adequacy(+)	.32	.06
Health factor(+)	.12	.02
Leisure interests(+)	.54	.02
Life satisfaction(−)	.27	.01
Retirement attitude(+)	.09	.16

[a]*Analysis based on about 605 working or voluntarily retired men aged 64–69 in 1975. Consequences tested but found not significant include worry about finances, formal organization activities, social-family, social-friends, solitary-sedentary, and satisfaction with activities. See also note to Table 6.5.*

and it shows a slight positive effect: the RHS health factor improves with an R^2 increase of .02 (Table 6.10).

Activity. There were several positive effects of voluntary retirement on various activities. The RHS shows that leisure interests increase (Table 6.10) and the DSLS shows that solitary activity, activity with friends, and household work activity all increase (Table 6.11). There were no significant effects on the other measures of activity.

TABLE 6.11
Significant Consequences of Voluntary Retirement among DSLS Men and Women[a]

Consequence	Total R^2 without Voluntary Retirement	R^2 Increase for Voluntary Retirement
Income(−)	.54	.04
Solitary activity(+)	.21	.04
Friends activity(+)	.13	.01
Household work(+)	.02	.04
Negative affect(+)	.25	.01

[a]*Analysis based on about 201 working or voluntarily retired men and women aged 52–76 in 1976. Consequences tested but found not significant include psychosomatic symptoms, self-rated health, hours spent relaxing, time spent in self-care, time spent in organizations, anomie, locus of control, future orientation, age identification, social worth, uselessness, life satisfaction, positive affect, and affect balance. See also note to Table 6.5.*

Attitudes. There were also several positive effects of voluntary retirement on satisfaction. The NLS showed small increases in leisure satisfaction and life satisfaction (Table 6.9). The RHS showed a small increase in life satisfaction and a large improvement in retirement attitude (R^2 increase = .16, Table 6.10). The DSLS showed no significant effects on most attitude measures. The one exception, negative affect, is so small an effect as to be negligible. The affect balance, which takes into account both negative and positive affect, shows no significant difference.

Thus in summary, it is clear that voluntary retirement had no substantial negative effects (even when there was income loss, it was balanced by greater income adequacy), but did have some net positive effects in the areas of activity and attitudes.

SUMMARY

Persons retiring because of poor health were a relatively deprived group before retirement. Those retiring for other compulsory reasons were relatively better off and those retiring for voluntary reasons were the most fortunate retirees. Similarly, those retiring for poor health suffered more negative consequences from their retirement, those retiring for other compulsory reasons suffered less, and those retiring for voluntary reasons enjoyed several positive effects. These differences among types of retirees were somewhat greater among the early retirees.

Thus, the reasons for retirement do make substantial differences in both the antecedents and consequences of retirement.

7
Work after Retirement

In this chapter our focus is on postretirement employment. We will explore the extent to which this occurs; examine which factors differentiate the working retired from the fully retired and from nonretired persons; and examine the personal impact of postretirement employment.

PREVIOUS RESEARCH ON WORK AFTER RETIREMENT

Retirement is not necessarily synonymous with work cessation. However, there is little information on the proportion of people who work after retiring and the amount of work that they do, for most figures on labor force participation do not report the retirement status of the worker. As yet no information on postretirement employment based on a nationally representative sample seems to have been reported. Such information on postretirement employment as is available tends to focus on people in particular occupations (e.g., retired professors, the majority of whom tend to work after retiring, see Fillenbaum & Maddox, 1974 and references there; Kell & Patton, 1978; or pension-favored automobile workers, of whom very few work after retiring, see Barfield & Morgan, 1969; Stagner, 1979).

There has been concern to identify both the environmental and personal factors which permit and encourage postretirement employment, as well as those factors which have the reverse impact. Probably uppermost are considerations of health, occupation, availability and adequacy of private pension and of social security, and attitudes to work and retirement (e.g., Gordon

& Blinder, 1980; Rhine, 1978). Also relevant is a change over time in the relative importance of different types of industries (Graney & Cottam, 1981).

Certainly, to the extent that health determines the sheer feasibility of working, it enters as an important consideration. Totally incapacitating physical and mental health may eliminate the possibility of working in all but rare instances. Health condition, however, should not be considered in isolation from the job, for different jobs have different health demands. It is, however, the rare study which provides information on the work potential of the individual and the capacity requirements of available jobs (see, for instance, Kelleher & Quirk's 1973 annotated bibliography).

Certain occupations tend to encourage continued employment. These include occupations which are much in demand (e.g., medicine) and which can be pursued on a self-employed basis. They tend to be upper level occupations, although with the changing national occupational structure we would expect service occupations to be heavily represented also. This, in turn, suggests that those who work after retirement come from the economic extremes. That is, there will be overrepresentation from those at the top and those at the bottom of the economic ladder. Those at the top are more often able to work and those at the bottom more often need to work. Certainly 1960 Census data indicate that those working at a later age (their retirement status is not reported) were most likely to come from these groups (Fillenbaum, unpublished analysis).

The effect of retirement pensions seems to depend on whether the source is social security or a private pension. Social security has been considered by some to be an inducement to continued employment (at least until age 65 and now perhaps beyond this, see, e.g., Blinder, Gordon, & Wise, 1980), and by some to be an incentive to retirement (e.g., Boskin, 1977; Burkhauser & Tolley, 1978). Private pensions, however, are largely inducements to retirement, and may place severer restrictions on postretirement employment than does social security with its earnings test (e.g., Clague, Palli, & Kramer, 1971; Quinn, 1981; Schiller & Snyder, 1982). Obviously, a pension in retirement will result in increased retirement income. Since income adequacy may be an important determinant of postretirement employment, it is difficult to determine to what extent cessation of paid employment after retirement reflects pension-related restrictions, or adequate economic status.

Attitude to work and to retirement have been seen as important determinants of continued employment, as well as of adjustment to retirement. It is expected that people who are committed to their work will be more likely to try to continue to work, while those who are not should prefer to cease working. The consideration that the latter might prefer alternative work, and if they found it might continue working, has not been explored. Similarly, those with a positive view of retirement are expected to welcome it, perhaps indeed to hasten it. This, however, is simplistic, and there is ample evidence indicating that the relationship between employment, retirement, and attitudes to each is more complex (e.g., Fillenbaum, 1971a; Goudy, Powers, & Keith, 1975).

Thus a variety of interrelated factors may predict employment at a later age or after retirement. Primary among these are socioeconomic status, health, adequacy and source of retirement income, characteristics of the job, and attitude to work and to retirement. In looking at predictors of work after retirement we shall examine each of these characteristics.

COMPARISONS

Our primary focus is on postretirement employment. In order to better understand this phenomenon, members of this group will be compared with members of two other similar age and same sex groups: those who have not yet retired, and those who have retired and *not* returned to work. These comparisons should enable us to identify the important characteristics of each group, and the unique characteristics of the working retired. We wish, however, to go further than seeing which predictors differentiate these three groups. We would also like to determine whether the behavior of each group has an impact on well-being. In the chapter "Consequences of Retirement" we examined the impact of retirement on the economic status, health, attitudes, and activities of respondents. The same categories will be examined here. Since the employment status of the working retired falls in between the status of the not retired and the fully retired, we would expect the well-being of the working retired to be generally intermediate between the well-being of the other two groups.

Most studies of retirement have been on men. Not only have there been few studies of women's retirement (see Chapter 8, "Gender Differences," and Szinovacz, 1982), but even fewer of work after retirement among female retirees. We will analyze separately data for both men and women, although because of sample size the analyses of women will be more restricted than those of men.

DATA SETS

The Retirement History Survey is the one data set analyzed for this chapter. Relevant data from the National Longitudinal Surveys (Mature Men) have already been analyzed by Parnes and Nestel (1981); while Boskin (1977) analyzed data from the Panel Survey of Income Dynamics (PSID); and information from the Duke Work and Retirement Study has been reported by Fillenbaum (1971b). The RHS is the only large data set providing information on both men and women in which the consequences of working after retirement could be examined.

SAMPLE

We are interested in three groups of persons: the retired who later work; the retired who do not work; and similar age members of the labor force who are not retired. Only persons working a minimum of 16 hours a week at baseline were eligible for inclusion. To become a member of the working retired group, subjects had to retire in either 1971 (wave 2) or 1973 (wave 3) and had to have worked after retiring and prior to 1975 (wave 4, the final wave examined). Those retiring in 1971 or 1973 who did no further work by 1975 were allocated to the nonworking retired group. Persons who, on all four waves (1969, 1971, 1973, 1975) said that they were not retired constituted the nonretired group. In some comparisons, persons who first retired in 1975 are included as nonretirees. Because of cost considerations, analyses were run on a one-third random sample.

CLASSIFICATION AS RETIRED

In the larger study of which this is a part, three definitions of retirement were used: a subjective definition, and two objective definitions based on hours worked (and pension receipt where that information was available). Since the objective definitions may not distinguish the unemployed and part-time nonretired from the retired, we have used the subjective definition in these analyses. All persons who said that they were fully or partly retired were classified as retired. Table 7.1 shows, separately for men and women, the numbers of persons retiring on each wave of the study, and of those retiring, the number and percent who reported working after retirement.

FINDINGS

In 1971, of those who had retired since 1969 over a third of the men (37%) and a quarter of the women (26%) worked during the following two years. In 1973 of those who had retired since 1971, 27% of the men and 22% of the women worked after retiring. Thus, those retiring at older ages were less likely to return to work. On average the men worked for 66 weeks in the two years following retirement while the women worked between 75 weeks and 80 weeks. In comparison, those who did not retire during the first four waves worked an average of 100 weeks between 1971 and 1973, and 95 to 96 weeks between 1973 and 1975. Thus, as expected, those working after retirement worked fewer weeks than those not retiring.

The data on men and women indicate that, while women are somewhat less likely to continue to work after retiring than are

TABLE 7.1
Number of Persons Retiring by 1975, 1973, or 1971
by Later Work Status and Sex ($N = 1845$)

	Men		Women		N^a
Did not retire	293		79		372
Retired 1973–1975	320		86		406
Retired 1971–1973	477		104		581
No work after retirement		346	73%	81	78%	
Worked after retirement		131	27%	23	22%	
Retired 1969–1971	369		105		474
No work after retirement		231	63%	78	74%	
Worked after retirement		138	37%	27	26%	

[a] *12 persons not classified because of incomplete information.*

men, those women who do work after retirement tend to work more weeks in the year. For both men and women the variance in extent of working is substantial, indicating that there are large differences in the amount of time devoted to work after retiring.

The data have been analyzed in two ways: by focusing on the work, and by focusing on the worker. Analysis of the work examines whether particular characteristics of the job or of retirement are related to postretirement employment. Included is further information on the amount and type of work actually performed. Analysis of the worker seeks to determine which personal characteristics distinguish the working retired from both the nonworking retired and the nonretired, and examines how postretirement employment affects later adjustment.

FOCUS ON THE WORK

Of the men who worked after retiring (there were too few women to permit meaningful analysis) nearly half worked for more than 100 weeks in the two years after retiring (i.e., they worked all year long). This level of effort was sustained for at least four years after retirement (see top panel, Table 7.2).

Information on whether this work was full-time or part-time was only analyzed from those at work at the time of the survey. The amount of missing data is, however, small (see bottom panel, Table 7.2). Between 30% and 48% worked full-time (40 hours or more a week), while between 17% and 35% worked half-time or less. The number of hours worked decreased as the retirees grew older.

These data indicate that between 11% and 17% of the retired men continued in year-round full-time employment. While the others worked less, very few worked for only a brief period of time.

Parnes and Nestel (1981), reporting on the postretirement work experience of NLS men who retired between 1966 and 1975, indicate that 17% of the white males and 15% of the black males were employed in the 1976 survey week. This undoubtedly underestimates the percentage who worked after retiring since it omits consideration of those who returned to work after retiring but were not working during the survey week. Nine percent of the whites and 6% of the blacks had worked the entire previous year (a smaller percentage than found for RHS) while between 34%

TABLE 7.2
Amount Worked by Retirees (Men Only)

	Retired in 1971				Retired in 1973	
	Work in 1971–1973		Work in 1973–1975		Work in 1973–1975	
Weeks worked	N	%	N	%	N	%
0	351		361		462	
1–25	10	(8)	12	(11)	8	(7)
26–52	24	(20)	17	(15)	23	(19)
53–75	7	(6)	8	(7)	10	(8)
76–100	24	(20)	21	(19)	28	(24)
>100	58	(47)	55	(49)	50	(42)
Hours worked/week at current job[a]						
0	349		349		460	
1–18	21	(17)	27	(22)	42	(35)
19–39	45	(36)	51	(41)	53	(44)
40	22	(18)	14	(11)	17	(14)
>40	37	(30)	33	(26)	19	(16)

[a]*Information only available from those holding a job at the time of interview.*

(blacks) and 40% (whites) worked full-time (35 hours) or more. The smaller percentage of retired NLS respondents working year-round may reflect the poorer health status of the NLS sample. Both studies agree that a significant proportion of those who work after retiring do so full-time and year-round.

Members of the RHS sample who were working part-time in 1975 were asked why they were working part-time. The most frequent response was that they were retired (42% of 1971 retirees, 46% of 1973 retirees); 18% (1971 retirees) and 25% (1973 retirees) named social security restrictions; 21% (1971) and 12% (1973) cited economic conditions; and 14% (1971) and 12% (1973) cited health and old age. This suggests that many could work more, but were not interested in doing so. Social security earnings limitations, which are frequently considered to have a restrictive effect on continued employment, apparently play a lesser role here.

Because of suggestions that occupational status tends to drop toward the end of the work life (Wentworth, 1968) the postretirement occupation of those working at the time of the interview was compared with the occupation of the job they had held when first seen (Table 7.3). With a single exception (the men who retired in 1971) the majority had a retirement job with the same status as their preretirement job. Such changes as did occur, however, were more likely to result in holding a lower status job. The extent to which this decline in status is attributable to retirement is, however, questionable. The ratio of change to lower versus change to higher occupational status jobs among not retired men is 1.6, as compared with 1.6 to 2.8 among the working retired males. The findings for women are similar, but caution must be exercised in interpretation because of their small numbers. These data confirm that there tends to be some decline in occupational status as working life draws to an end. This decline may be, but is not necessarily, more frequent among the retired.

Although stability of employment was lower among the working retired than among the not retired, the majority remained with the same employer over the two-year periods. More than two-thirds of the working retired remained with the same employer after retirement. By comparison 92% of those not retired remained with the same employer between 1973 and 1975.

We also checked whether persons retiring from certain occupations were more (or less) likely to work after retiring (Table 7.4). While on average 32% of the men report postretirement employment, only 11% of non-farm laborers but 58% of farmers and farm managers continue to do work. (There were too few retired women to permit analysis.) In general, the lower status occupations (non-farm laborers and operatives) had lower proportions working after retirement. An exception to this generalization are the professional and technical workers who also had a lower proportion (26%) working after retirement.

A comparison of the timing of retirement with postretirement employment (Table 7.5) indicates that postretirement employment is more likely among early (under age 65) or on time (age 65) retirees than among late retirees. This relationship is particularly noticeable among the women, among whom none of those retiring late continued to be employed. These data suggest that early retirement does not necessarily mean departure from the labor force and show that late retirees are more likely to retire completely. Finally, 25% of men working after retirement are self-employed, compared with 10% self-employed among nonworking retirees (8% and 3% respectively for women). Thus, self-employment appears to encourage work after retirement.

TABLE 7.3

For the Employed, Change in Occupational Status Since 1969, by Time of Retirement (Percentages)[a]

	Retired in 1971 Occupation in		Retired in 1973 Occupation in		Retired in 1975 Occupation in		Not retired Occupation in	
	1973	1975	1973	1975	1973	1975	1973	1975
Men (N)	104	95	109	102	311	76	284	281
Occupation								
Higher	20	20	14	19	11	12	9	11
Same	48	38	56	51	72	54	76	70
Lower	31	42	30	30	17	34	14	18
Ratio lower:higher	1.6	2.1	2.1	1.6	1.5	2.8	1.6	1.6
Women (N)	25	19	18	22	82	15	75	78
Occupation								
Higher	8	5	6	5	6	0	7	6
Same	84	79	83	86	83	100	81	81
Lower	8	16	11	9	11	0	12	13
Ratio lower:higher	1.0	3.2	1.8	1.8	1.8	1.0	1.7	2.2

[a]Data only from persons employed at the time of interview.

TABLE 7.4
Percentage of Retired Men Working by Baseline Occupation

	% No work	% Work	N
Service employees	66	34	74
Farm laborers	65	35	17
Non-farm laborers	89	11	53
Operatives	73	27	155
Craftsmen	70	30	212
Sales and clerical	65	35	77
Farmers and farm managers	42	58	57
Managers and administrators (non-farm)	64	36	125
Professional and technical	74	26	73
N	576	267	843
%	68	32	

In summary, these data show that roughly a third of the men and a quarter of the unmarried women retiring in the early 1970s continued to work after retiring, nearly half of them working full-time. Employment was stable for the majority and at the same occupational level as their preretirement jobs. For all workers, both the retired and nonretired, when occupational status changed it

TABLE 7.5
Timing of Retirement by Work After Retirement

Timing of Retirement	Retired Men		Retired Women	
	No Work	Work	No Work	Work
Early				
N	358	166	111	35
%	68	32	76	24
On time				
N	190	95	36	15
%	67	33	71	29
Late				
N	29	8	12	0
%	78	22	100	0
Total				
N	577	269	159	50
%	68	32	76	24

was more likely to be in a downward than in an upward direction. Such change was somewhat more frequent among the working retired. Those who retired late were less likely to return to work than others. Farmers and farm managers were the most likely to work after retirement, perhaps because continued self-paced employment was more feasible for them. Although it has been suggested that people at the occupational extremes are more likely to work after retirement or to continue to work to a later age, in the mid-seventies it was the self-employed and those in upper-occupational status positions who were the most likely to work after retirement. Perhaps the increased adequacy of Social Security income and the availability of Supplemental Security Insurance have increased the attractiveness of full retirement, and reduced employment forced by dire necessity (cf. Boskin, 1977).

FOCUS ON THE WORKER

Who are these people who work after retiring? How do they differ from those who do not work after retirement and from those who do not retire?

In earlier analyses we grouped the antecedents of retirement into five categories. Then, using multiple measures within each category (to the extent available) we tried to determine the additional contribution made by successive categories in predicting retirement. The categories were analyzed in the following logical sequence: demographic, socioeconomic, health, job characteristics, attitudes to work and retirement. To maintain comparability these categories are also used here. However, our present interest is in determining whether these characteristics distinguish the working retired from the nonworking retired and the nonretired. Therefore we will first compare the three groups in terms of these characteristics. Then, using discriminant analysis, we will see to what extent it is possible to predict membership in each of the three groups. Finally, since we are also interested in the consequences of these three employment statuses, we will compare adjustment in four selected areas.

Table 7.6 lists, for each of the five categories, those measures which distinguish the working retired from either the nonworking retired or from the nonretired. The number of significant differences found is greater for men than for women, which may in part be attributable to the smaller size of the female sample.

TABLE 7.6
Comparison of Working and Nonworking Retired and Nonretired, by Sex

	Men			Women		
	Retired		Not Retired	Retired		Not Retired
	Working	No Work		Working	No Work	
N	269	577	293	50	159	79
Demographic						
Age						
Mean	60.7[f]	60.6	59.5	60.4[e]	60.5	59.8
S.D.	1.7	1.7	1.7	1.6	1.7	1.6
Race						
% Black	9	8	7	12	9	9
Socioeconomic						
Education						
Mean	9.7[f]	9.7	11.2	10.2	10.6	10.3
S.D.	3.4	3.4	3.8	2.6	3.1	2.7
Occupational status						
Mean	5.5[e]	5.2	6.0	4.3	4.4	4.8
S.D.	2.3	2.3	2.3	2.6	2.8	2.7
Income adequacy						
Mean	4.1[c]	4.6	4.6	3.8[a]	4.3	4.3
S.D.	1.6	1.4	1.4	1.5	1.5	1.4
No. dependents						
Mean	1.4[a]	1.3	1.5	.1	.1	.2
S.D.	1.1	1.0	1.1	.5	.30	.5

Socioeconomic factor						
Mean	$1.7^{a,f}$	2.3	2.8	1.0^e	2.0	2.6
S.D.	3.4	3.2	3.4	3.5	3.7	3.0
Health						
Health factor, baseline						
Mean	3.3^f	3.3	2.2	2.6	3.1	2.1
S.D.	2.9	2.9	2.1	2.5	2.9	2.1
Job characteristics						
Hours work/week, 1969 job						
Mean	47^c	44	48	38	39	40
S.D.	13	10	14	9	8	6
Pension available						
% available	45^c	64	48	28^b	47	39
Years worked at longest job						
Mean	22^a	23	21	14	16	14
S.D.	12	11	11	10	11	10
Total years worked						
Mean	44^c	41	43	29	30	32
S.D.	7	9	5	14	14	14
Self-employed						
% self-employed	25^c	10	25	8	3	4
Attitudinal						
Retire if lose current job						
% retire	26^f	31	11	22^d	34	9
Intend to retire						
% retire	75^f	84	59	56^a	72	51

(continued)

TABLE 7.6 (Continued)

	Men			Women		
	Retired		Not Retired	Retired		Not Retired
	Working	No Work		Working	No Work	
Participation in formal organizations						
Mean	11.6^f	11.8	15.6	7.1^d	8.3	9.3
S.D.	13.6	9.1	8.4	3.9	6.4	7.1
Social contacts, friends						
Mean	7.6^b	6.9	7.3	7.9	8.3	7.7
S.D.	3.8	3.8	3.5	3.4	4.0	3.4

$^a p < .05$
$^b p < .01$ } Refers to comparisons between working and nonworking retired.
$^c p < .001$

$^d p < .05$
$^e p < .01$ } Refers to comparisons between working retired and nonretired.
$^f p < .001$

Demographic

On average, the working retired are about a year older than the nonretired. They do not differ significantly by age or race from the nonworking retired.

Socioeconomic

Compared to the nonretired men, the working retired had less education, lower occupational status, less adequate income, and a poorer socioeconomic status. Their income and socioeconomic status was also poorer than that of the nonworking retired, while the numbers of dependents they had was greater. These findings suggest that work after retirement often reflects a need for additional income.

Among women only two of these findings are supported: the poorer income and lower socioeconomic status of the working retired.

Health

The health of the working retired men is similar to that of the other retirees, but poorer than that of the nonretired. No significant differences were found for the women. This indicates that some decline in health need not prevent work after retirement.

Job Characteristics

The working retired had worked more hours per week before retirement than the nonworking retired. Although the total number of years they had worked since age 21 was greater (by three years) than that worked by the nonworking retired, they had spent fewer years at their longest job. More importantly only 45% compared with 64% of those who were fully retired had estimated that a pension would be available, and 25% compared with 10% were self-employed. There were no significant differences in these characteristics between the male working retired and nonretired. Differences in pension availability were found for the women, but the other differences did not reach statistical significance.

Attitudes to Work and Retirement

Fewer of the working retired compared to the fully retired intended to retire if they lost the job held at baseline. Indeed, fewer intended to retire at all. Compared to the nonretired the working retired belonged to fewer formal organizations (which might reflect their poor socioeconomic status) but, compared to those who did not work after retirement, they maintained more contact with friends. With the exception of contacts with friends, similar findings hold for the women.

Information on work commitment (figures are not reported in the table) was first obtained on the second wave (1971) and is only available for persons employed at that time. The three groups did not differ in extent of work commitment—a rather unexpected finding.

DISCRIMINANT ANALYSES

Those variables which distinguished the working retired men from either of the other two groups were entered into a discriminant analysis (women were not analyzed because of small numbers). This permitted us to determine which variables were important in discriminating among these three groups, and the extent to which group membership could be accurately predicted. The variables are listed, by major category, in Table 7.7, where order of entry is also listed. The analysis was done twice, once using an F value of 3.80 as the cutoff criterion (a minimum value), the second time using an F value of 20.00 (a more stringent criterion). Comparison of the results of these analyses permit us to determine the extent to which classification is impaired under a more parsimonious model.

Nine of the 17 available variables entered under the less restrictive model, the first four of which enter into the more parsimonious model. These variables in order of importance are: age, the intention to retire, number of years worked, level of education, whether self-employed, health status, retirement intention, income adequacy, and number of hours worked per week on the job held at baseline.

It is of interest that occupational status does not enter (perhaps because of its correlation with education) and that the availability of a pension is inconsequential (perhaps because

TABLE 7.7
Variables Available for and Selected by the Discriminant Analyses Comparing Working Retired, Nonworking Retired, and Nonretired Men

| | | Order of Selection of Variables | | | |
| | | Analysis 1 | | Analysis 2 | |
	Variables Available	Order	F Value	Order	F Value
Demographic	Age	1	50.39	1	50.59
	Race				
Socioeconomic	SES factor				
	Income adequacy	8	6.27		
	Occupational status				
	Education	4	21.66	4	21.16
	No. of dependents				
Health	Health factor	6	16.47		
Job characteristics	No. hours work/week	9	4.63		
	Pension available				
	No. years at longest job				
	No. years worked	3	24.23	3	24.48
	Whether self-employed	5	17.94		
Attitudinal	Retire if lost job	7	7.00		
	Intend to retire	2	39.18	2	37.56
	Membership in formal organizations				
	Social contacts with friends				

number of years worked and self-employed status are already present).

The ability of these variables to discriminate among the three groups is poor. The nine-variable model accurately classifies 40% of the working retired, 57% of the nonworking retired, and 71% of the nonretired. The more parsimonious four-variable model is almost equally efficient (or inefficient), correctly classifying 54% of the working retired, 46% of the nonworking retired and 70% of the nonretired (Table 7.8). The main difference between the two models lies in their capacity to distinguish between the two types of retirees. The data indicate that the retired can be more accurately distinguished from the nonretired, than the workers from the nonworkers. For the nine-variable model, 78% of the retired and 71% of the nonretired are correctly classified, com-

TABLE 7.8
Classification by Each Discriminant Analysis of
Working and Nonworking Retired and Not Retired

| | Percent of Group Classified as | | | |
	Working Retired	Nonworking Retired	Not Retired	N
	Analysis Based on Nine Variables			
Actual group				
Working retired	40.4	32.8	25.5	261
Nonworking retired	20.6	57.3	22.0	567
Not retired	17.5	12.3	70.2	285
	Analysis Based on Four Variables			
Actual group				
Working retired	54.0	18.1	27.9	265
Nonworking retired	28.2	46.3	25.4	570
Not retired	20.9	9.1	70.0	287

pared with 78% of the workers and 57% of the nonemployed. The figures for the four-variable model are similar: correct classification of 74% (retired) and 70% (nonretired) compared with 87% (workers) and 46% (nonworkers). A plot of the mean weighted scores places the scores for the two retired groups in close proximity, each being a similar distance from the mean score of the nonretired. This graphically suggests that the two retired groups are more similar to each other than to the nonretired.

In order to determine more clearly which variables distinguished between the two different types of retirees (those who would work after retiring and those who would not) and the two different types of workers (those who would work after retiring and those who would not have retired), separate discriminant analyses based on the same pool of variables were run. From this pool the variables which were statistically important in identifying members of the first pair overlapped minimally with those important in identifying members of the second pair.

A combination of three variables, age, education, and the intention to retire, accurately identified 74% of those who would work after retiring and 71% of those who would not. The further addition of four statistically significant variables (health, extent of socializing with friends, participating in formal organizations, planning to retire if the current job is lost) resulted in little further improvement in identification. Those who would work after retiring were younger, had received fewer years of education, and had less intention of retiring.

In the second comparison (between those who would work after retiring and those who would not have retired), only two variables were important—whether self-employed, and the number of years worked since age 21. These variables correctly identified 87% of those still not retired six years later, but misclassified 68% of those who would work after retiring. The addition of three further variables (years worked at the longest held job, income adequacy, extent of socializing with friends) reduced the misclassification of the future working retired from 68% to 46% but also reduced the percentage of accurately identified nonretirees from 87% to 71%. When considered individually, only one of these five variables (income adequacy) showed a statistically significant difference between the two groups of workers.

These data indicate that there are more readily identifiable differences between those who will work after retiring and those who will not, than between those who will retire but still work and those who will not retire. Compared with those who will fully retire, those who will work in retirement are younger and less privileged, and consider retirement less attractive. They, like those who will not retire within the next six years, have a substantial commitment to work and while they are less likely than those who will fully retire to receive work-related rewards in the form of a pension, the feasibility of being employed continues to be available, and for those who will work after retirement the financial necessity to work is present also.

CONSEQUENCES OF WORKING AFTER RETIREMENT

With the exception of its depressing effect on income our present studies show that retirement *per se* rarely has a severe negative impact. Nevertheless, there are some studies of specialized groups which show that paid employment after retirement has a beneficial effect. Carp (1968), for instance, found that paid work (as compared to volunteer work) has a positive impact on self-esteem and social relationships, while Soumerai and Avorn (1983) report a higher level of perceived health and life satisfaction among part-time retired employees than among controls. It therefore remains an empirical question as to whether working after retirement is more beneficial than remaining fully retired, and whether work has the same impact, regardless of retirement status.

To investigate this matter we examined outcome in four areas: economic, health, activities, and attitudes. We wanted to determine to what extent outcome six years after baseline, i.e., in 1975, could be explained in terms of postretirement employment.

Residualized change regressions were run. Baseline status on the variable in question was entered first (column 1, Table 7.9), then all other statistically significant and theoretically relevant measures taken at baseline (column 2), and finally a code for work

TABLE 7.9

Impact of Working after Retirement: Comparisons of
Working Retired with Nonworking Retired and Nonretired Workers

	R^2 Initial Status	R^2 All but Type of Worker	R^2 Increase in Comparison of Working Retired with	
			Nonworking Retirees	Nonretired Workers
Economic				
Income adequacy	.24	.35		-.08[a]
Socioeconomic factor	.55	.57	+.01[b]	-.03
Health				
Health factor	.13	.17	+.03	-.02
Activities				
Formal organizations	.50	.54	+.01	
Extra-work interests	.50	.52		+.01
Attitudes				
Life satisfaction	.24	.30	+.01	-.01
Attitude to retirement	NA[c]	.04	-.01	+.06
Attitude to work	NA	.00	+.01	
Satisfaction with activity level	NA	.08	+.02	

Neither work nor retirement status help to explain extent of participation in solitary or sedentary activities, seeing friends or family, or worrying about money.

[a]- Working retired in poorer position than comparison group.

[b]+ Working retired in better position than comparison group.

[c]NA-Not available.

status (column 3) or retirement status (column 4) was entered. Thus, we ran an analysis in which the final variable referred to (1) work status (comparing the working retired, coded 1, with the fully retired, coded 0), or (2) retirement status [comparing the working retired (1) with nonretired workers (0)]. Statistically significant results are presented in Table 7.9.

If working after retirement has no unique effect, then the final variable entered should not have a statistically significant impact (in column 3). If, however, working has an effect, postretirement employment should have explanatory power, and its impact should be positive if work has the desirable effects suggested by some studies. Further, in the latter case the ordering from most to least desirable condition should reflect extent of employment, i.e., nonretired, working retired, fully related.

Our findings tend to support this hypothesis. Where socioeconomic status, health, life satisfaction, and attitude to retirement are concerned, postretirement employment helps explain variance in outcomes. With the exception of attitude to retirement, where the impact is reversed, postretirement employment has a positive impact when comparison is with the fully retired, and a negative effect when comparison is with the not retired. That is, after other relevant baseline characteristics have been taken into account, work after retirement does have an effect such that the working retired are better off than the fully retired, but not as well off as the nonretired.

In terms of participation in formal organizations, attitude to work, and satisfaction with activity level, variance in outcome is explained by postretirement employment only when comparison is made with other retirees. Again, the working retired are in a favored position. In two other areas, income adequacy and extra-work interests, work after retirement helps explain outcome only when comparison is made with nonretirees. The working retired have more extra-work interests, but their income adequacy is lower. It is important to note that post-retirement employment did not help explain variance in income adequacy when comparison was made with the fully retired. This suggests that the income generated by such work may help to equalize income adequacy among the retired, but is not enough to increase it over that of the fully retired. This further suggests that many of those who work after retiring do so out of need. At baseline those who would later work had less adequate incomes. Among the working retired, lower occupational status persons (service workers) are over-represented and upper level persons are underrepresented. This is in disagreement with data from the Duke Work and Retirement Study (Fillenbaum, 1971b) where upper occupational status people were more likely to work after retiring. It should be recalled that the age range of the present RHS sample is 64 to 69 in 1975. Professionals, who tend to retire late, may not yet have retired and consequently would not be in the working retired group. Reanalysis using final wave (1979) data, when respondents will be aged 68 to 73, would help clear up this issue.

Although present data suggest that postretirement employment is beneficial, it must be emphasized that these workers are a self-selected group. Compared to the other retirees they experienced fewer constraints on working and a greater need to do so, for more were self-employed and fewer were in receipt of a pension. Based on such a self-selected sample it is not appropriate to recommend postretirement employment for all. Neither may these data be used to indicate that continued employment without retirement is necessarily beneficial.

Nevertheless, these data do show that among those aged 64 to 69 in 1975, the working retirees were better off compared to the fully retired in terms of the socioeconomic factor, the health factor, formal organizations, and several attitude measures, even after all relevant initial characteristics were controlled. Similarly, the nonretired workers were better off than the working retirees in terms of income adequacy, the socioeconomic factor, the health factor, and life satisfaction.

SUMMARY

We have found that substantial proportions of retired men and women (from about a quarter to over a third) returned to work, that men were more likely than women, and that younger retirees were more likely than older retirees to return to work. While there were large variations in the amount of work after retirement, nearly half of the retired men worked all year long, and between a third and a half worked full-time. Thus, postretirement employment is a frequent and substantial phenomenon among retirees.

The majority of working retirees had a job with the same status as their preretirement job, but there were somewhat more downward shifts in status than upward shifts. Farmers and farm managers and the self-employed were most likely to return to work, while non-farm laborers were least likely to do so.

Bivariate comparison of those who worked after retirement with those who did not indicated that the former had had a poorer socioeconomic status. Although they had been in the labor force longer, and worked more hours a week at baseline, they were less likely to receive a pension. More, however, were self-employed. Somewhat fewer intended to retire. Thus, those who would work after retirement had a strong attachment to the labor force and an increased possibility of continued employment, but they were less likely to have received substantial financial rewards from working. Postretirement work income could well affect their economic well-being in retirement. The importance of these variables was confirmed by discriminant analyses.

Residual change analysis found that, controlling for all relevant initial characteristics, the working retired were better off compared to the fully retired in terms of a socioeconomic measure, health, formal organization participation, and several attitude measures. Similarly, the nonretired workers tended to be better off in these outcomes than the working retired. Thus it appears that working after retirement allows a person to enjoy some of the benefits of both retirement (increased leisure) and of employment (income supplementation, health maintenance, and satisfaction).

8
Gender Differences

Retirement typically is viewed as a major transition of later life. Common sense, as well as social science theory, suggests that departure from the labor force involves several consequential changes with implications for individual attitudes and behaviors. Among the possible changes resulting from retirement are loss of income, loss of a structure and routine for daily activity, loss of interaction with co-workers who may have become important sources of social support, loss of social status and prestige, loss of a major foundation upon which personal identity rests, and loss of an avenue for attaining the satisfaction of accomplishment and productivity (cf. Friedmann & Havighurst, 1954). In spite of the seemingly obvious truth of this perspective, most recent studies of retirement suggest that departure from the labor force has little observable impact upon retirees—and that those changes that can be attributed to retirement are as likely to represent positive as negative outcomes (cf. George & Maddox, 1977; Palmore, Fillenbaum, & George, 1984; Streib & Schneider, 1971).

In light of the lack of fit between theoretical expectations and research findings about the impact of retirement, several authors have suggested that an important agenda for retirement research is specification of the conditions under which retirement does and does not lead to negative outcomes and/or identification of the subgroups for whom the retirement transition is differentially difficult (cf. George, 1980, Sheppard, 1976). If one takes these suggestions seriously, it is immediately apparent that there are multiple conditions and/or subgroups that might be compared for evidence that retirement has differential antecedents and consequences. Subgroups based on gender, race, socioeconomic status,

An earlier version of this chapter appeared in the *Journal of Gerontology*, 1984, *39*, 364–371. Used by permission.

and marital status are obvious possibilities for comparative analysis. Factors (rather than subgroups) that might be hypothesized to condition the retirement transition include attitudes toward and personal investment in work, family structure, and levels of social support.

The purpose of this chapter is to compare the antecedents and consequences of retirement among men and women. An examination of gender differences in the retirement transition is needed because (1) most previous studies, especially longitudinal studies, focus exclusively on men; (2) there have been multiple calls for increased study of retirement among women; (3) labor force participation rates among women have increased dramatically, thus increasing the need for knowledge about retirement among women; and (4) the fragmentary available evidence about gender differences in retirement is both contradictory and intriguing.

THEORETICAL ISSUES AND PREVIOUS RESEARCH

Literature addressing gender differences in the retirement transition is scant in volume and ambiguous in results. There are several reasons for the ambiguity characteristic of previous findings. First, precisely because the volume of previous research is low there is not a sufficient knowledge base to provide cumulative findings. Second, as is often the case with a relatively unexplored research topic, most studies of women's retirement have been based on samples of limited size and representativeness and cross-sectional research designs (Szinovacz, 1982). A third and more theoretical issue concerns choice of an appropriate comparison group for understanding women's retirement. Some studies take the approach used in this chapter: comparing the retirement transitions of women and men (cf. Atchley, 1982; Newman, Sherman, & Higgins, 1982; Streib & Schneider, 1971). Other studies compare retired women with older housewives (cf. Fox, 1977; Jaslow, 1976; Keith, 1982). Information generated by these two types of studies is very different. Comparisons of men and women highlight the impact of gender (or its correlates) upon the retirement process. Comparisons of retired women and older housewives provide information about the persisting effects of labor force participation upon older women. Thus these two types of studies do not provide comparable information. Because this chapter compares retirement among men and women, this literature review will focus primarily upon research comparing men and women.

In general previous research comparing men's and women's retirement suggests that there are few gender differences (cf. Atchley, 1982; Gratton & Haug, 1982; Newman et al., 1982; Streib & Schneider, 1971). In particular, previous literature suggests that both men and women typically adjust well to the retirement transition (Gratton & Haug, 1982). The evidence for this assertion rests on studies that use life satisfaction or a related construct as the criterion of adjustment. Although we do not disagree with this conclusion, retirement potentially affects multiple outcomes, and life satisfaction is not the only outcome of interest or importance. In this chapter, we examine multiple outcomes—health, income, activities (time spent in personal hobbies, household tasks, organization participation, and interaction with family and friends), self-concept dimensions, and subjective well-being—and compare the effects of retirement upon these outcomes for both men and women.

Further, although both men and women typically exhibit satisfactory levels of subjective well-being subsequent to retirement, available literature suggests other types of gender differences in the retirement transition. Streib and Schneider (1971) found that retirement increased feelings of uselessness for both sexes, but that the increases were significantly greater for women. This finding challenges the common stereotype that work has less salience for women than men. This stereotype also is challenged, albeit less directly, by evidence that, prior to retirement, women anticipate more problems during retirement than men (Atchley, 1971b; Newman et al., 1982). Streib and Schneider also report that retirement increases the probability of self-identification as old for both men and women, but that women are more likely than men to maintain a "younger" age identity.

Two recent studies suggest that women and men engage in different types and amounts of retirement preparation. Newman, Sherman, and Higgins (1982), in a study comparing retirement among professionals, found that men had more positive attitudes toward retirement and had made more retirement plans than women. Kroeger (1982) has performed perhaps the most comprehensive examination of gender differences in retirement preparation to date, although the sample was local (New York City) rather than national. Kroeger examined both formal (i.e., structured retirement preparation programs) and informal (i.e., talking to others and seeking information through the media) retirement preparation experiences by preretirees. The findings indicated that women were more likely than men to engage in no retirement preparation. Among those preretirees who engaged in retirement planning, women were more likely than men to participate in formal programs. In contrast, men were more likely than women to engage in informal retirement preparation. Moreover, education and gender interacted to influence patterns of retirement preparation. Among the highly educated, both men and women exhibited similar and relatively high rates of retirement preparation. Among the less educated, however, men typically used informal sources of retirement preparation and women typically did not participate in any retirement preparation. The results of these studies suggest that men and women exhibit different patterns of participation in retirement preparation experiences. A note of caution is merited, however. As yet, there is no evidence that retirement preparation has long-term impact on adjustment to retirement (cf. Glamser, 1981; Glamser & DeJong, 1975).

Atchley (1982) has performed perhaps the most comprehensive comparison of gender differences in the retirement process to date. Although the sample used in this study is local rather than national, the sampling was systematic and the restricted sample is counterbalanced by the scope and richness of the data in the study. Atchley examined three stages of the retirement process: the preretirement period, the retirement transition, and the post-retirement period. Modest gender differences were found at all three stages of retirement. The major difference at the preretirement stage was that women were more likely than men to indicate no plans to retire. The major difference during the retirement transition was that levels of social activity decreased significantly more for female than male retirees (although in absolute terms women were more active than men both before and after retirement). The gender differences were most complex at the post-retirement stage. At that stage, although men and women did not significantly differ in terms of absolute levels, the predictors of life satisfaction and attitudes toward retirement were different for men and women. Based on these findings, Atchley concludes that there are significant differences in the retirement transition for men and women. He also puts this conclusion in perspective, however, by pointing out that, overall, men and women both adjust very well to the retirement transition.

One area of research based on samples of only women merits brief review. A number of investigators have suggested that retirement may have more adverse consequences for women than men because women are more likely than men to have interrupted work histories and women tend to be segregated in a narrower range of occupations and industries than men (and these occupations are characterized by relatively low wages and decreased likelihood of pension coverage). Two studies provide important data bearing on this issue. O'Rand and Henretta (1982) examined the impact of work history variables upon the estimated retirement incomes of married and unmarried women. The results indicate that, net of other factors, interrupted work history (especially late entry to the labor force), employment in a lower status occupation, and employment in a peripheral industry are independently and significantly related to estimated retirement income. These results suggest that women's work histories are important predictors of financial status during retirement, although a major limitation of the study is that the dependent variable is expected rather than actual retirement income. In another study, Block (1982) examined the impact of women's work histories upon life satisfaction during retirement. The results indicated that net of other predictors, continuous versus intermittent work history was not significantly related to life satisfaction of retirees. Further research on this topic clearly is needed. These studies, however, suggest that women's work histories are related in a significant and expected way to retirement income but may not have broader effects on other indicators of retirement adjustment.

Although gender differences in retirement is an attractive research topic, the subject also poses certain theoretical and methodological difficulties. Why should one anticipate gender differences in the antecedents and consequences of retirement? One could argue that there is little reason to believe that gender *per se* is inherently likely to affect the retirement transition. Using this logic, gender—like age, race, and several other basic demographic and personal characteristics—may be best viewed as a proxy for a number of underlying biological and psychosocial processes. If significant sex differences are observed, this may reflect failure to include or measure all of the appropriate processes and variables that are associated with gender in our society. In spite of these problems of attribution of variance to gender and its correlates, however, it is important to examine sex differences in the retirement transition. Male and female labor force participants differ in many ways and these differences may be associated with differential antecedents and/or consequences of retirement. The approach taken in this chapter is to interpret observed gender differences (after inclusion of theoretically relevant controls) as simply differences in the way the retirement transition is experienced by men and women in American society. We do not claim that the observed differences represent intrinsic concomitants of gender.

In this chapter the antecedents and consequences of retirement are compared by performing separate analyses of men and women from the same data sets. In contrast to many previous studies, this chapter is based on relatively large and representative samples and utilizes longitudinal data. Rigorous sample selection criteria are applied so that the analyses permit comparisons within gender groups (of those who do and do not retire), across gender groups, and across surveys. These multiple bases of comparison, as well as the inclusion of multiple outcomes, permit a relatively comprehensive examination of gender differences in the retirement transition.

This chapter emphasizes issues of prediction. In the analyses predicting retirement, we wish to know whether the same variables that predict retirement for men also predict retirement for women. In the analyses that examine the consequences of retirement, we wish to know whether the impact of retirement (i.e., both the direction and the strength of its relationship with various outcomes) is the same for men and women. We do not attempt to trace the complex causal processes that specify the retirement transition. Rather, our purpose is to generate an overall assessment of the degree to which the antecedents and consequences of retirement are similar for men and women.

In the analyses presented in this chapter, retirement is related to seven classes of variables: demographic characteristics, job characteristics and attitudes, health, finances, social activity, self-concept, and subjective well-being. The seven classes of variables were selected on the basis of previous theory and research concerning the correlates of retirement. Although the vast majority of past work has been based on exclusively male samples, it is reasonable to hypothesize that these variables might affect and be affected by retirement among both men and women. One additional conceptually relevant class of variables would be family and household responsibilities. Such factors might be especially important correlates of women's participation in and departure from the labor force. The fact that such factors previously have not been examined as correlates of retirement probably reflects the fact that most previous studies examined retirement among men. Unfortunately, measures of family and household responsibilities were not included in the data sets available for analysis.

METHODS

Data Sources

Only two of the data sets used in this project included sufficient numbers of women to permit meaningful comparisons of gender differences in the antecedents and consequences of retirement: the Retirement History Study (RHS) and the Duke Second Longitudinal Study (DSLS).

As described previously, RHS started with a nationally representative sample of 11,153 men and unmarried women aged 58 to 63. To reduce computer costs, most of the analyses were performed on a one-third random subsample. In order to be included in the analyses reported in this chapter, respondents had to meet the following criteria: (1) present in both the 1969 (baseline) and 1975 (outcome) test dates, (2) have been employed at least 16 hours a week in 1969, and (3) have declared that they were not retired in 1969. These selection criteria were used in order to restrict the sample to those respondents for whom longitudinal data were available and to compare those who became retired during the course of the study with those who remained in the labor force. Use of the one-third sampling strategy and application of the selection criteria resulted in a sample of 1845 respondents: 1468 men and 377 women.

Because the RHS sample design included all men but only unmarried women, preliminary analyses were performed to determine whether the men should be analyzed as a single group or split into married versus unmarried. These preliminary analyses indicated that men's marital statuses were irrelevant for examination of the antecedents of retirement, but had important implications for understanding the consequences of retirement. Thus, for the RHS, analyses of the antecedents of retirement were based on a comparison of men and women, but analyses of the consequences of retirement were based on comparing women, married men, and unmarried men.

The Duke Second Longitudinal Study (DSLS) was conducted by the Duke University Center for the Study of Aging and Human

Development. Respondents were tested on four occasions; the modal years of data collection were 1969, 1971, 1973, and 1975 (the same dates as RHS interviews). The baseline sample consisted of 502 men and women aged 46 to 70. The sampling frame consisted of participants in a local health insurance plan. The same selection criteria that were described for the RHS were applied to DSLS participants, resulting in a subsample of 156 men and 79 women for use in these analyses.

Measures

Eight classes of variables were extracted from each survey for analysis of gender differences in retirement: the seven classes of variables described previously and measures of retirement. In order to maximize comparisons, measures were selected and/or recoded to be as similar as possible across the two surveys. This effort was modestly successful, but some variables were measured in substantially different ways in the RHS and DSLS. The measures used in this chapter are described briefly below; detailed descriptions of the measures are provided in the Appendix.

Demographic Variables. The demographic characteristics of respondents were measured identically in the two data sets. Age was measured in years, education was measured as years of formal schooling, and household size was indexed by the number of people in the household. In both data sets, marital status was measured as a dichotomous variable, with 0 indicating nonmarried and 1 representing being married. Empirical checks indicated that the various reasons for being unmarried were not significantly related to the dependent variables of interest; thus, the simple dichotomous variable was sufficient for our purposes. In the RHS, race was operationalized as a dichotomous variable with 0 representing white respondents and 1 representing black participants. The few RHS respondents who reported another racial identity were omitted from analysis. All DSLS participants were white.

Job Characteristics and Attitudes. In both RHS and DSLS, occupation was measured using the nine-category first-digit Census Bureau Occupation codes. Otherwise, the two surveys included substantially different measures of job characteristics and attitudes. The RHS included several other job-related variables. Pension plan participation was a dichotomous dummy variable, with 1 representing pension coverage. Years worked in longest job and

years worked since age 21 also were included in the RHS. Two
attitudinal variables were available in the RHS, both measured as
dichotomous dummy variables. Respondents were asked whether
they would retire if they lost their job (1 = yes) and whether they
planned to retire in the future (1 = yes). The DSLS also included
two dichotomous attitudinal items. Respondents were asked
whether they preferred work or leisure (1 = prefer work) and whether they would work if they didn't have to (1 = would work even
if didn't have to).

Health. The RHS included a four-item health limitations scale,
with higher scores representing increased health limitations. The
DSLS included two health measures. The first required respondents to rate their health along a four-point scale ranging from
"poor" to "excellent." The second health-related measure was
a psychosomatic symptom list from the Health Opinion Survey
(MacMillan, 1957).

Finances. Household income measures were available in both
surveys, but measured differently. In the RHS, income was reported in actual dollar amounts. In the DSLS, income was measured along a continuum of nine ordinal categories. Both surveys
included information about the number of dependents who were
supported by the household income. One additional income measure was included in the RHS. A measure of income adequacy
was developed by adjusting household income by the number of
dependents, scaling the metric to the Intermediate Budget of the
U.S. Department of Labor. Finally, the RHS also included a single-
item measure concerning the frequency with which respondents
worried about their financial situations.

Activities. Both surveys included several measures of activity,
although the measures were minimally comparable. In the RHS,
multi-item scales were used to measure participation in formal
organizations, time spent in extra-work interests (including home
maintenance and personal hobbies), interaction with family, time
spent in solitary activities, and interaction with friends. The RHS
also included a single-item attitudinal measure of satisfaction with
activities.

The DSLS included an activities inventory that generated information about the amount of time each month spent in the following types of activities: participation in voluntary organizations,
interaction with family, interaction with friends, household tasks,
personal hobbies, sedentary activities, self-care activities (e.g.,
bathing and grooming), and church attendance.

Self-concept. The RHS included no measures of self-concept. The DSLS included measures of three self-concept dimensions. Age identification was measured as a dichotomous dummy variable with 1 representing self-identification as old. The DSLS also included two multi-item self-concept scales: self-perceptions of social worth and self-perceptions of uselessness.

Subjective Well-being. The RHS included a 4-item scale measuring satisfaction with life as a whole. The DSLS included multiple measures of subjective well-being and related concepts. Anomie was measured using a 9-item scale (McClosky & Schaar, 1965). Locus of control was measured using an 11-item scale (Jessor et al., 1968), coded such that higher scores represented increased internality. Overall life satisfaction was measured using the Cantril Self-Anchoring Scale (Cantril, 1965). Finally, three measures were based on the Affect Balance Scale (Bradburn, 1969): amount of positive affect, amount of negative affect, and ratio of positive to negative affect.

Thus, we cast a fairly wide net in terms of including measures potentially related to retirement. Some measures proved to be significant antecedents and/or consequences of retirement; others were unrelated to departure from the labor force. The decision to be relatively inclusive was predicated on the belief that it is important to identify those factors that are and are not related to retirement.

Retirement. One of the emphases of the larger retirement study on which this chapter is based is a comparison of alternative methods of defining and operationalizing retirement. Three major definitions were compared: objective retirement, subjective retirement, and amount of employment. Respondents were considered to have objectively retired if, by the end of the study, they were employed less than 35 hours a week and were receiving a public or private pension. Thus, persons who were working full-time were not considered retired, even if they were receiving pension income. Similarly, unemployed persons without retirement pensions were not considered retired. There were very few respondents in the latter category because most older workers are eligible for some type of pension when they stop or substantially reduce their employment. Subjective retirement was based solely on respondents' self-reports of their employment status: respondents were considered retired if they said they were retired (regardless of whether they had jobs or received pensions). Amount of employment is a reverse measure of retirement and has the advantage of being a continuous variable. In the RHS, amount of retirement was based on hours worked in the past two years. In the DSLS, amount of employment could only be approximated in that the only information available was whether respondents were working full-time, part-time, or not at all.

In the analyses reported in this chapter, the retirement measure used had virtually no effect on the findings. For purposes of convenience and brevity, the retirement variable reported is objective retirement, which is interpretively easier to handle than the counterintuitive measure of amount of employment and is a conceptually more rigorous definition than subjective retirement. Using the objective definition, 74% of the men and 76% of the women in the RHS retired during the course of the study. In the DSLS, 60% of the men and 54% of the women retired during the course of the study. The lower rates of retirement in the DSLS reflect the fact that DSLS participants were about three years younger, on average, than RHS participants.

Method of Analysis

The analyses examine gender differences in both the antecedents and consequences of retirement. The overall strategy was to perform separate analyses for men and women within the two data sets and to compare the results across both gender groups and data sets. In the analyses examining the antecedents of retirement, baseline measures of the seven classes of variables were used to predict the likelihood of retirement among men and women. In the analyses of the consequences of retirement, factors that are potentially affected by retirement and that were measured at the last test date were related to retirement, net of the baseline levels of the outcome variables and other relevant control variables. All analyses were longitudinal and the independent and dependent variables were measured at different times, thus clarifying temporal order.

Predicting who does and does not retire involves a dichotomous dependent variable. The use of ordinary least squares (OLS) regression to predict dichotomous dependent variables may lead to inefficient regression coefficient estimates and predicted values of the dependent variable that fall outside of the metric values of 0 and 1 (Cox, 1978). Logistic regression is a preferable technique for predicting dichotomous dependent variables. The logistic regression procedure calculates maximum likelihood estimates for the parameters of a model. The logistic regression tables presented in this chapter include the antilogged coefficients (AC) for independent variables in the models. The antilogged coefficient represents the estimate of how a one unit change in the independent variable multiplies the odds of scoring a 1 on the dependent variable (i.e., in this case, of becoming retired). Antilogged coefficients of one or greater increase the odds of becoming retired; antilogged coefficients of less than one decrease the odds of retiring. The overall fit of the logistic model is assessed by R. The R statistic is similar to the multiple correlation in OLS regression after a correction is made for the number of parameters estimated. Individual R statistics also are available for each independent variable. R values range from -1 to +1 and the absolute value of the R indicates the relative contribution of each independent variable to the overall model fit. The signs attached to the R statistics for the independent variables simply indicate whether the coefficients increase or decrease the odds of scoring 1 on the dependent variable (in this case, the probability of retiring).

The analyses addressing gender differences in the consequences of retirement utilize continuous dependent variables and ordinary least squares regression. We wish to identify the variables that change as a result of retirement and to describe the direction and strength of those changes. In these analyses, all dependent variables are factors that are potentially affected by retirement and all are measured at the last test date. Hierarchical regression equations are used to determine the degree to which retirement affects these outcomes net of other factors. In the hierarchical regression equations, the baseline measure is entered in the first step, other Time 1 predictors are entered into the equation next, and the retirement measure is entered into the equation last. This strategy permits us to determine whether retirement has a significant impact upon the outcome measures net of other significant predictors.

FINDINGS

Gender Differences in the Predictors of Retirement

Tables 8.1 and 8.2 present the logistic regression equations that best predict retirement among men and women in the RHS and DSLS respectively. Both tables are restricted to statistically signifi-

TABLE 8.1
Significant Predictors of Objective Retirement
among Men and Women in RHS (Logistic Regression)[a]

Time 1 Predictors	Men		Women	
	AC[b]	R	AC	R
Age	1.78	.29	1.59	.25
Education	.92	-.08		
Occupational status	.88	-.08		
Health limitations	1.95	.08		
Pension coverage	2.32	.14		
Years in longest job	1.02	.09		
Years worked since age 21	.96	-.07		
Total R		.40		.27

[a] All coefficients reported are statistically significant (p ≤ .05).
[b] AC = Antilogged coefficient.

cant predictors ($p < .05$). Among RHS men, older age, lower education and occupational status, greater health limitations, being enrolled in a pension program, greater tenure in longest job, and fewer years worked since age 21 significantly increased the odds of retiring during the study. Most of these predictors are expectable and have been reported in previous literature. The single ex-

TABLE 8.2
Significant Predictors of Objective Retirement
among Men and Women in DSLS (Logistic Regression)[a]

Time 1 Predictors	Men		Women	
	AC[b]	R	AC	R
Age	1.41	.32	1.29	.36
Income	1.99	.19		
Contact with friends	1.12	.12		
Work if didn't have to	.09	-.11		
Self-rated health	.43	-.09		
Total R		.48		.48

[a] All coefficients reported are statistically significant (p ≤ .05).
[b] AC = Antilogged coefficient.

ception is the finding that fewer years worked since age 21 was associated with increased likelihood of retirement. At first glance, this finding appears anomalous in that a shorter work history should be associated with lower pension equity, lower occupational status, and so forth. It should be noted, however, that the coefficient for years worked since age 21 is net of these predictors. Perhaps a shorter work history reflects lower levels of occupational commitment, controlling on other factors. Among the DSLS men, older age, higher income, increased interaction with friends, reporting that one would not work unless necessary, and perceptions of poorer health significantly increased the probability of retirement.

The only significant predictor of retirement for women in both samples was age. The older the respondent, the more likely that she retired over time. The gender differences are quite striking. There are multiple significant predictors of retirement for men and only a single significant predictor for women. These results suggest that the predictors of retirement differ considerably for men and women and that other kinds of variables need to be examined as possible predictors of retirement among women.

Gender Differences in the Consequences of Retirement

Tables 8.3 and 8.4 summarize the significant effects of retirement for the outcomes available in the RHS and DSLS respectively. The tables are restricted to only significant effects of retirement ($p \leq .05$). As noted previously, for the RHS, separate results are presented for married men, unmarried men, and women. The tables present the significant R^2 increments contributed by the retirement variable and the total R^2 of the equations from which the net R^2 values were extracted. Tables 8.3 and 8.4 summarize 51 regression equations; an additional 21 equations were calculated in which the retirement variables were not related to the dependent variables for any gender group. Explication of the full equations for all these dependent variables is beyond the scope of this chapter and is not necessary in that we are interested in the net effects of retirement.

Table 8.3 indicates that retirement was significantly related to six outcomes for RHS married men, net of other variables. Retirement was associated with increased health limitations, decreased

TABLE 8.3
Significant Retirement Effects among Men and Women in RHS[a]

Dependent Variable	Married Men R^2 Increment	Married Men Total R^2	Unmarried Men R^2 Increment	Unmarried Men Total R^2	Unmarried Women R^2 Increment	Unmarried Women Total R^2
Health limitations (+)	.01	.18				
Income (−)	.01	.20	.05	.29	.03	.23
Income adequacy (−)	.02	.37	.06	.39	.05	.41
Formal organizations (−)	.00	.53				
Extra-work interests (+)	.01	.51			.01	.56
Life satisfaction (−)	.00	.31				

[a]Dependent variable included only if retirement had a significant effect for at least one group. All R^2 increments reported are statistically significant (p ≤ .05). Pluses and minuses indicate positive and negative associations with retirement.

TABLE 8.4
Significant Retirement Effects among Men and Women in DSLS[a]

Dependent Variable	Men R^2 Increment	Men Total R^2	Women R^2 Increment	Women Total R^2
Psychosomatic symptoms (+)	.03	.26	.02	.29
Self-rated health (−)	.04	.29		
Income (−)	.17	.46		
Time spent in hobbies (+)	.02	.10	.20	.36
Time spent in self-care activity (+)	.04	.20		
Time spent with friends (+)	.03	.18	.04	.19
Time spent in household tasks (+)	.08	.17	.04	.10
Frequency of church attendance (+)	.04	.48		
Perceptions of self-worth (+)	.04	.36	.08	.40
Perceptions of uselessness (+)	.11	.28		
Locus of control (+)			.04	.21

[a]Dependent variable included only if retirement had a significant net effect for at least one group. All R^2 increments reported are statistically significant (p ≤ .05). Pluses and minuses indicate positive and negative associations with retirement.

income and income adequacy, decreased participation in formal organizations, increased time spent in extra-work interests, and decreased life satisfaction. Retirement also was related to decreased income and income adequacy for both unmarried men and for women. In addition, for women, retirement was related to increased time spent in extra-work activities. Retirement was not related to contact with friends, interaction with family, or time spent in solitary activity for any of the gender groups. Retirement was related to considerably more outcomes for married men than for unmarried men or women, net of other variables.

Table 8.4 demonstrates that retirement was related to more outcomes for men than for women in the DSLS also. For men, retirement was related to increased psychosomatic symptoms; decreased perceptions of health; decreased income; increased time spent in hobbies, self-care, household tasks, and with friends; increased frequency of church attendance; increased perceptions of social worth; and increased perceptions of uselessness. For women, retirement was associated with increased psychosomatic symptoms, increased time spent in hobbies and household tasks, increased time spent with friends, increased perceptions of social worth, and increased perceptions of internal control. For both DSLS men and women, retirement was unrelated to participation in formal organizations, interaction with family, time spent in sedentary activities, age identification, anomie, life satisfaction, and the three affect measures.

It also is important to examine the magnitude of the retirement effects in general and in terms of gender differences. Although all of the retirement effects reported are statistically significant, the magnitudes of the R^2 increments often are quite small. Thus we should pay special attention to those outcomes for which the retirement effects are relatively large. In the RHS, the retirement variable explained about 5% and 3% of the variance in the decreased income and 6% and 5% of the variance in decreased income adequacy among the unmarried men and women, respectively. The remainder of the retirement effects in the RHS were quite small in magnitude. In the DSLS, the R^2 increments contributed by the retirement variable generally were stronger than in the RHS. For men, retirement had a very large impact upon income, explaining a net variance of 17.3%. Also for men, retirement explained a large proportion of the increases in perceptions of uselessness (net R^2 = 10.7%). In contrast, retirement was unrelated to both income and perceptions of uselessness for women. Retirement had a much stronger impact upon time spent in hobbies for women than for men (net R^2 of 20.0% for women, compared to 1.5% for men).

DISCUSSION

The purpose of this chapter was to examine gender differences in the antecedents and consequences of retirement. For men, the significant predictors of retirement include age, pension coverage, various aspects of work history, preretirement socioeconomic status (i.e., occupation, education, income), and, to a lesser extent, work-related attitudes. These results are not surprising—most previous studies report similar results, although relatively few previous studies include longitudinal data, careful screening criteria for sample selection, and multivariate statistical techniques. In terms of the consequences of retirement, our findings suggest that, for men, retirement impacts most strongly upon health, income, some types of activities (especially time spent in personal hobbies and household tasks), and feelings of uselessness. Again, similar findings have been reported in previous research (cf. Mutran & Reitzes, 1981; Streib & Schneider, 1971). In contrast, comparable analyses did a very poor job of predicting retirement among women (age was the only significant predictor) and retirement was related to substantially fewer outcomes for women than for men.

There are two general explanations possible for the gender differences observed in this paper. One possibility is that women's work histories and patterns of labor force participation are so varied that it is not possible to identify common predictors and consequences of retirement. One might argue that current cohorts of older women typically have not pursued occupational careers that are characterized by the regularity and predictability typical of men. For these cohorts of women, it might be argued, occupation took a secondary role to family responsibilities. Consequently, both entry into and departure from the labor force is less predictable and less consequential than for men. Although there is no evidence to decisively refute such a position, we do not find this line of reasoning compelling for two reasons. First, in both the RHS and DSLS, approximately equal proportions of men and women retired during the data collection period. Given the comparable age ranges of men and women within both studies, it appears that retirement rates are nearly identical for men and women. In this sense, retirement is not less predictable for women and men. Rather, the results suggest that prediction of individual differences in retirement behavior is less successful among women than among men. Second, the overwhelming majority of RHS women were unmarried. (All were unmarried at the time the sampling frame was developed; a small proportion of women married during the study.) The arguments about irregular work histories are far less applicable to unmarried than married women.

A second potential explanation for the gender differences in the antecedents and consequences of retirement is that we need a different theoretical foundation for understanding men's and women's retirement. The theoretical orientations and previous research used to select the pool of variables included in our analyses largely addressed retirement among men. It is possible—and, indeed, given our results, likely—that the major factors that explain individual differences in retirement behavior among women were not included in the analyses. An important agenda for future effort will be identification of the variables that predict individual differences in retirement patterns among women. Initial efforts should focus upon theoretical development and qualitative research to identify potential explanatory factors. Use of complex causal models to trace the retirement process will be important future efforts. Specification of such models, however, requires better understanding of the factors related to women's retirement.

The results of this study suggest that retirement has beneficial as well as detrimental consequences for both men and women. In the DSLS, retirement was associated with increased psychosomatic symptoms for both men and women. Retirement was associated with decreased income for all RHS participants and for DSLS men. The finding that retirement did not significantly decrease income for DSLS women may reflect the fact that the vast majority of these women were married. In such cases, household income may be less likely to exhibit significant decreases subsequent to retirement. The remaining negative retirement effects were less generalizable. For RHS married men, retirement also was associated with increased health problems, decreased participation in formal organizations, and decreased life satisfaction. For DSLS men, retirement was related to decreased levels of self-reported health and increased feelings of uselessness.

The remaining retirement effects were generally positive in orientation. For RHS married men, RHS women, DSLS men, and

DSLS women, retirement was associated with increased time spent in personal hobbies and household tasks. DSLS men and women also exhibited increased interaction with friends after retirement. In addition, DSLS men increased time spent in self-care activities and frequency of church attendance. Although departure from the labor force inevitably alters daily routine, most retirees apparently expand their commitments to other types of activities to fill the available time. Retirement also has interesting positive effects upon some attitudinal variables. Both DSLS men and women exhibited significant increases in feelings of social worth subsequent to retirement. This multi-item scale included perceptions of being respected, competent, and valuable. In addition, DSLS women reported increased perceptions of internal locus of control and RHS men reported higher life satisfaction after retirement. Thus, although retirement impacts upon fewer outcomes for women than men, positive effects are observed for both sexes.

This chapter began with the premise that an important arena for retirement research is examination of differential patterns of retirement among specific subgroups. Although the primary focus of this chapter is gender differences, the findings suggest that marital status also may be an important factor affecting the retirement transition. Because of the sampling frame used, marital status was inherently confounded with gender in the RHS. Empirical evidence indicated that marital status was irrelevant for the analyses predicting retirement but consequential for the analyses of the effects of retirement. It is interesting that the effects of retirement were very similar for unmarried men and women (the vast majority of whom were unmarried) in the RHS. Although decreased income and income adequacy were associated with retirement for all RHS participants, married men displayed a considerable number of additional significant retirement effects. Ideally we would have liked to compare the antecedents and consequences of retirement in four groups: married men, unmarried men, married women, and unmarried women. Unfortunately, these comparisons were not possible in either data set. As noted previously, the RHS included insufficient numbers of married women. In the DSLS, which had a relatively small sample size, 93% of the men and 89% of the women were married. Thus, neither data set permitted rigorous sex and marital status comparisons. This issue, however, should be an important area for future research.

Several authors have pointed out the need to devote increased attention to the ways in which multiple roles interact across the life course (cf. Fiske, 1980; George, 1982). Currently, family life typically is examined exclusive of other social roles, occupational careers are studied without information about the other roles that workers enact, and so forth. Hogan (1980) and Marini (1978) recently examined the timing of multiple role transitions during early adulthood. These works represent important initial efforts to document the significance of role configurations in a given life stage, but much more work is needed. If the marital status differences in patterns of retirement that are suggested in this study can be documented as stable and meaningful, the retirement transition may be an excellent context for future examinations of the interactions of multiple roles during later life.

9
Racial Differences

In recent times there has been increasing recognition of the diversity present among the aged and of the lack of information on minority status and aging (e.g., Fujii, 1980; Gelfand & Kutzik, 1979). Our concern in this chapter is with one of the largest minority groups in our society: black males. Our focus is retirement, a time considered to have particular importance to older workers. Are the predictors and consequences of retirement the same or different for black males and white males? The cohort we studied was born between 1906 and 1912. The present data reflect their status in 1975–1976, when they were 64 to 69 years old.

White males have enjoyed a privileged position in our society. While certain white ethnic and religious groups have experienced educational and occupational discrimination, this has been comparatively short-lived, and pales beside the discrimination experienced by blacks (Jencks, 1983; Sowell, 1981). Such discrimination has resulted in a median of only seven years of schooling for the age cohort from which our black sample is drawn. This is over three years less than the median for all persons their age (U.S. Department of Commerce, 1976, Table 198). In addition, they have had to contend with pervasive job discrimination, even more than recent cohorts. The average occupational status of blacks is substantially lower than that of whites, their income from employment is less, they are less likely to be in jobs which offer private pensions, and even when they are in such jobs they seem less likely to receive those pensions (Thompson, 1979). Such conditions can be expected to have an important impact on retirement.

An earlier version of this chapter will appear in the *Journal of Gerontology*. Used by permission.

Countering these earlier detrimental effects, the late 1960s and early 1970s saw a remarkable improvement in the rights of workers and the financial status of the elderly. Laws against sex, race, and age discrimination in employment were passed and enforced (see review by Daymont, 1981). The mandatory retirement age was raised. Employment among blacks and continued employment among older workers was facilitated (Abbott, 1980; Daymont, 1981). Beginning in 1969, Social Security retirement benefits were increased and indexed to the cost of living. In 1974, Supplemental Security Insurance (SSI) was introduced, and the proportion of older persons below the poverty level started to approximate that for the general population. The enactment of the Employee Retirement Income Security Act in 1974 brought with it greater assurance of pension receipt for those in covered employment (Rodgers, 1981), providing further financial security. The workers of this cohort were retiring into a more financially secure situation than did earlier retirees.

Thus, this particular cohort was at a historical turning point. Their employment years reflected the impact of race and age discrimination, and while the deleterious effects of these might carry over into their retirement years, it should be ameliorated by the recently improved financial situation.

We have suggested that retirement could be predicted by a combination of five categories of variables. These, in causal order, were: demographic characteristics, socioeconomic status, health, job characteristics, and attitudes. Each was expected to have a direct effect on retirement, as well as indirect effects through subsequent categories.

This model was useful in explaining retirement among males, although the explanatory contribution of the different types of variables differed according to the way in which retirement was defined and the age at which retirement occurred.

Given previous findings on the predictors of retirement, and what we know regarding certain group differences between black males and white males, we expected that the set of retirement predictors for blacks would be different from that for whites.

Specifically, for blacks we expected that only those basic characteristics related to keeping a job would be important, i.e., age, socioeconomic status, and health. For whites, however, we expected a broader range of variables to be important, because they have enjoyed greater opportunity to choose work which reflects their capacities and interests. For whites work should be better integrated into their lives and consequently hold more meaning. So for whites, all five categories were expected to be important, i.e., demographic, socioeconomic, health, job characteristics, and attitudes.

Within each category, however, we expected previous findings to hold. That is, we expected retirement to be more likely among those who were older, of lower socioeconomic status, in poorer health, had a pension available, and held a positive view of retirement (e.g., Bixby, 1976; Palmore, 1971; Parnes, 1981; Schwab, 1976; Sheppard, 1976; Streib & Schneider, 1971).

The impact of certain preretirement circumstances, particularly poorer jobs, lower income, and reduced likelihood of receiving a private pension, may continue to be felt after retirement. Because of this, we expected the effects of retirement on black males to be different from that on white males.

The socially integrative role of work (Friedmann & Havighurst, 1954) is little evidenced among persons in lower occupational positions (Wilensky, 1960). We expected the cessation of work to be less disruptive for the latter because the lives of lower occupation workers are less integrated around their work. Thus retirement was expected to have less impact on blacks, because more blacks were in lower status occupations.

However, most findings indicate that occupational status and income are positively related to adjustment after retirement (e.g., George & Maddox, 1977; Simpson & McKinney, 1966; Stokes & Maddox, 1968; Thompson, 1958; Thompson & Streib, 1958). In explanation, it is posited that the capabilities resulting in improved occupational status and income also aid in adjustment to retirement. While for whites there may be a positive relationship among personal capability, occupational status, and income, this relationship may be weaker among blacks because of discrimination. But further, discrimination goes beyond the workplace, extending into the social arena. Not only is their work less likely to act as a socially integrative force, but discrimination may force most blacks to develop a personal life which is distinct from their work lives.

It is possible that in this black cohort, status within their community is more closely related to simply having a job and to the stability of their income, than to the status of the job. Retiring from such a job should be less problematic than retiring from one in which there is strong personal investment, for the extrinsic rewards of such a job may remain (e.g., higher income from social security, community status) even as the disagreeable aspects (e.g., the lower status which the job implies) are left behind. Further, for those who were in unstable employment or not covered by some form of retirement pension (social security or other pension) the advent of SSI in 1974, shortly before the samples studied here were reinterviewed, may have meant that at last there was a stable, if minimal, income. For such persons, of whom a disproportionate number are black (*Social Security Bulletin*, 1982), retirement should not have as negative an impact.

In consequence, we expected the impact of retirement to be more negative for white males than for black males.

METHOD

Of the major longitudinal studies having substantial information on subjects before and after retirement only two included sufficient samples of blacks to permit analysis: These are the Social Security Administration's Retirement History Survey (RHS) and the National Longitudinal Surveys (NLS).

Only men were analyzed in order to eliminate the complications of gender differences. To facilitate comparisons between RHS and NLS, the men analyzed were all aged 64 to 69 on the final wave examined. Those from RHS were initially aged 58 to 63 (Wave 1, 1969), those from NLS were initially aged 54 to 59 (Wave 1, 1966). For RHS there was a 6-year and for NLS a 10-year interval between the initial and final waves examined here. The one-third RHS sample consisted of 1468 men, of whom 1351 (92%) were white and 117 (8%) black. The NLS sample consists of 975 men, of whom 708 (73%) were white and 267 (27%) were black because of a three-to-one oversampling of blacks. The two samples are described in Tables 9.1 and 9.2 in terms of those variables important in predicting retirement. Within each data set the black males are similar to the white males in age and health. Blacks have had less education, fewer are married, their occupational status is lower, and their financial status is poorer. Blacks also work fewer hours per week, and are less likely to be self-employed.

TABLE 9.1
Characteristics of Variables Which Are Significant Predictors of Retirement, by Race. RHS, Men only, Initial Age 58 to 63

	White		Black		
	Mean	S.D.	Mean	S.D.	t-test
Demographic					
Age	60.19	1.69	59.98	1.71	
Socioeconomic					
Education (years)	10.38	3.44	7.29	3.93	a
Occupational status	5.62	2.23	4.06	2.20	a
Income adequacy	4.56	1.43	3.43	1.56	a
Number dependents	1.33	.91	1.82	1.86	a
Health					
Health factor	2.90	2.72	2.95	2.68	
Job characteristics					
Pension	.57	.49	.41	.49	
Hours worked/week	45.73	11.68	43.69	8.64	c
Self-employed	.17	.38	.11	.32	d
Attitudinal					
If lose job retire	.23	.42	.15	.36	d
Intend to retire	.75	.44	.72	.45	
Proportion retired					
Subjective dichotomous	.80		.82		
Objective dichotomous	.75		.70		
N (maximum)	1351		117		

[a] $p < .0001$
[b] $p < .001$
[c] $p < .01$
[d] $p < .05$

Black RHS men have a better educational and financial status than do NLS blacks. These differences may reflect a higher labor force dropout rate at younger ages for less competent blacks (Daymont, 1981; Schwab, 1976).

In RHS 80% of the whites and 82% of the blacks were classi-

TABLE 9.2
Characteristics of Variables Which Are Significant Predictors of
Retirement, by Race. NLS, Men Only, Initial Age 54 to 59

	White		Black		
	Mean	S.D.	Mean	S.D.	*t*-test
Demographic					
Age	56.37	1.69	56.18	1.71	
Socioeconomic					
Education (years)	10.17	3.57	6.14	3.85	a
Poverty ratio	4.29	4.02	2.26	1.52	a
Wages (annual)	5951	5840	3524	2571	a
No. children <18	.37	.83	.74	1.41	a
Area unemployment	2.20	.68	2.42	.59	a
Job characteristics					
Pension	.51	.50	.37	.48	a
Hours worked 1966	1059	1191	806	1041	b
Other job in past 5 yrs.	.76	.43	.85	.36	b
Compulsory retirement	.34	.47	.34	.48	
Core industry	.48	.50	.52	.50	
Attitudinal					
Favor retirement	5.45	1.78	5.09	1.70	c
Extrinsic interest in job	.19	.40	.31	.46	a
Negative attitude to work	.26	.44	.28	.45	
Retirement definition (proportion retired)					
Subjective dichotomous	.67		.65		
Objective dichotomous	.80		.80		
N (maximum)	708		267		

[a] $p < .0001$
[b] $p < .001$
[c] $p < .01$
[d] $p < .05$

fied as subjectively retired on the final wave examined. However,
in NLS only 67% of the whites and 65% of the blacks were so
classified. This difference is due to the different questions asked
in the two surveys.

Similarly, the percentages of respondents objectively retired differs somewhat in the two studies, because the definitions had to be operationalized differently. In the RHS 75% of the whites and 70% of the blacks were classed as objectively retired. In the NLS the respective percentages were 80% and 80%, reflecting a more lenient standard (data on pensions were omitted).

Any predictor whose zero-order correlation with two of the three measures of retirement was significant for either blacks or whites was retained for further analysis. Since the sheer preponderance of whites could mask any differences due to race, separate analyses were run for blacks and for whites using an identical pool of potentially explanatory variables.

FINDINGS

Predictors of Retirement

Tables 9.1 (RHS) and 9.2 (NLS) provide descriptive information on those variables which entered the final equations. It should be noted that some variables did not enter some equations.

Comparison of the two data sets indicates that the variables in each category tend to be similar, with each data set contributing certain information not present in the other. On both RHS and NLS, blacks have a significantly lower status on each of the socioeconomic variables and on most of the job characteristics measures examined. Health was a significant predictor of retirement only for RHS. This probably reflects the more sophisticated measure of health available for RHS (a factor-derived scale, based on four items), as opposed to the single dichotomous measure in NLS.

The findings from examining predictors of the three alternative definitions of retirement are so similar that description will be restricted to one—the subjective dichotomous definition. Only notable departures by the other two definitions will be mentioned.

On RHS all 11 variables listed in Table 9.1 entered as significant predictors of retirement for the whites (Table 9.3). Only two variables were significant for blacks. A very similar pattern was found for NLS (Table 9.4). While seven predictors were significant for whites, only two were significant for blacks.

For RHS the total R (i.e., the overall fit of the model) for whites, based on all significant variables, was .36, a value very similar to that obtained for whites in NLS ($R = .34$). The specific contribution of each category to this final value varied by data set. R based on age was .20 for RHS but was .08 for NLS. The addition of socioeconomic variables increased R by .06 in RHS and by .08 in NLS, two very similar amounts. However, while health and job characteristics resulted in a further increase in R by .07 in RHS, the increase attributable to just the latter category was .13 in NLS. Attitudes contributed a similar amount in both cases (R of .03 for RHS, .05 for NLS).

Among white males those most likely to retire were older, and the relevance of age was not reduced by the addition of further explanatory variables; in fact it was slightly strengthened.

Of the four SES variables examined level of education was the most important for whites, those with more education being less likely to retire. More dependents also reduced the likelihood of retirement. However, the relevance of occupational status and income adequacy faded when job characteristics and attitudes were considered. In RHS, those in poorer health were more likely to retire. Job characteristics played a lesser role in RHS than in NLS. Those who were self-employed, who worked fewer hours per week initially, and who expected to receive a pension were more likely to retire (RHS). On NLS those who were in jobs where there was compulsory retirement, who had changed their jobs within the previous five years, and who were working in a core industry were more likely to retire.

Finally, attitudes had a distinct impact on retirement. On both RHS and NLS white males who intended to retire or who held positive views of retirement were more likely to retire.

Thus, for white males a diversity of characteristics were important in predicting subjectively assessed retirement.

In sharp contrast was the sparsity of variables which significantly predicted retirement for blacks, and the lack of agreement among these variables across the two data sets. On RHS only age and health were significant predictors for blacks, the former yielding an R of .32 while the two variables together provided an R of .49. These two variables alone better explained subjective retirement for black RHS males than did the 11 variables included in the analysis for white RHS males. In the NLS also, only two variables were important in explaining retirement for black males (level of education and changing jobs in the previous five years),

TABLE 9.3

RHS. Comparing Predictors of Retirement, by Race. Subjective definition of Retirement (Logistic Regression)

White Males ($N = 1343$)

	Demographic		Socioeconomic		Health		Job Characteristics		Attitudinal	
	AC[a]	R	AC	R	AC	R	AC	R	AC	R
Demographic										
Age	1.38	.19	1.40	.20	1.43	.21	1.46	.21	1.44	.20
Socioeconomic										
Education			.91	-.10	.91	-.09	.90	-.11	.90	-.10
Occupational status			.93	-.04	.93	-.04	1.00	.00	1.00	.00
Income adequacy			1.02	.00	1.05	.00	.93	.00	.91	.00
No. dependents			.85	-.04	.86	-.03	.84	-.05	.83	-.05
Health										
Health factor					1.14	.11	1.17	.12	1.14	.10

Table (hierarchical regression; AC = Antilogged coefficient)

Job characteristics

Variable	AC	β	AC	β
Pension available	1.55	.06	1.30	.01
Hours worked/week	.99	-.05	.99	-.03
Self-employed	.53	-.07	.51	-.07

Attitudinal

Variable	AC	β	AC	β
Intend to retire			2.15	.12
Retire if lose job			1.96	.07

Total R   .20   .26   .29   .33   .36

Black Males (N = 116)

Variable	AC	β	AC	β
Demographic				
Age	1.88	.27	2.02	.29
Health				
Health factor			2.88	.19

Total R   .32   .49

[a]AC = Antilogged coefficient.

133

TABLE 9.4
NLS. Comparing Predictors of Retirement, by Race.
Subjective Definition of Retirement (Logistic Regression)

	White Males (N = 671)							
	Demographic		Socioeconomic		Job Characteristics		Attitudinal	
	AC	R	AC	R	AC	R	AC	R
Demographic								
Age	1.14	.08	1.15	.09	1.17	.09	1.16	.08
Socioeconomic								
Education			.90	-.14	.89	-.15	.89	-.14
Job characteristics								
Other job in past 5 yrs.					1.87	.09	1.76	.07
Compulsory retirement					2.03	.10	2.06	.10
Core industry					1.75	.09	1.58	.07
Attitudinal								
Pro-retirement							1.24	.09
Negative attitude to work							1.85	.06
Total R	.08		.16		.29		.34	
	Black Males (N = 255)							
Socioeconomic								
Education			.93	-.09	.92	-.11		
Job characteristics								
Other job in past 5 yrs.					3.34	.17		
Total R			.10		.20			

but the total R was only .20. Thus, while a diversity of issues affected retirement among white males, only the most basic issues affected retirement among black males.

In the RHS the identical set of variables significantly predicted retirement for white males under the other two definitions of retirement. There was a slight change for blacks: instead of health, the intention to retire was important for the objective dichotomous definition, while four variables (age, education, self-employment status, and the intention to retire) were important in predicting continued participation in the labor force.

In the NLS there was some change with changing definitions of retirement in the variables important for white males. In predicting objective dichotomous retirement the poverty ratio became important (poorer people were more likely to retire) while job changing in the past five years became irrelevant. Prediction of continued participation in the labor force required 10 of the variables described in Table 9.2. The omitted variables were both attitudinal: negative attitude to work and extrinsic interest in the job.

Among black NLS males education became important in predicting objective dichotomous retirement, while prediction of continued participation in the labor force was based on age, education, wages, and number of hours worked at baseline. Continued work was more likely among younger, better educated, lower paid black men who worked more hours in 1966.

Consequences of Retirement

The consequences of retirement were grouped into four categories: economic, health, activities, and attitudes. Table 9.5 indicates the measures selected from RHS and from NLS. Measures were assigned to only one category, although some may logically fit in more than one category. Further information on these measures is provided in the Appendix.

We wished to determine whether retirement net of other variables had a differential impact on the two races. Table 9.6 (for RHS) and Table 9.7 (for NLS) displays the results of OLS multiple regressions, indicating the extent to which each measure of retirement contributed to an explanation of variance in the consequence measure after (1) baseline status on the consequence had been taken into account (where a baseline was available) and (2) all other relevant baseline measures had been taken into account. The other baseline measures included were those which on both theoretical and statistical grounds were related to the consequence.

Although our earlier work indicated that the definitions of retirement used here differed little in explanatory power, in order to increase rigor separate analyses were run for each definition and only when all three definitions of retirement yielded significant

TABLE 9.5
Specific Consequences of Retirement Examined in RHS and NLS

Category	RHS	NLS
Economic	(B)[a] Income adequacy (B) Socioeconomic factor	(B) Family income (B) Assets Receipt of SSI Receipt of food stamps
Health	(B) Health factor	Health limitation present (B) Combined health items
Activities	(B) Participation in formal organizations (B) Pursuit of solitary/sedentary activities (B) Extent of contact with family (B) Extent of contact with friends (B) Extra-work interests	
Attitudes	(B) Life satisfaction Attitude to retirement Attitude to work Satisfaction with activity level Worry about finances	Level of happiness re: House Area of residence Health Standard of living Leisure activities
Personal happiness		

[a]*(B) Baseline data available.*

results did we consider it appropriate to say that retirement was significantly involved. We considered the involvement of retirement to be more tentative when only one or two definitions yielded significant findings.

Data from both RHS and NLS indicated that retirement consistently had a significant impact only where economic matters, health, and attitude to retirement were concerned. However, retirement did not help explain all the aspects of economic status or health which were examined and it did not necessarily have the same impact on blacks as it did on whites.

Economic. The matters examined included family income, assets, receipt of SSI and of food stamps (all NLS), and family income, income adequacy, and a factor-analytic derived measure of socioeconomic status (RHS). Both baseline and final wave data indicated that for all variables examined blacks were in a poorer economic position than were whites.

The results of the regression analyses (Tables 9.6 and 9.7) indicated that retirement caused a significant drop in family income for whites and probably also for blacks. Retirement increased receipt of SSI among blacks but not among whites (of whom only 3% receive it) but did not influence receipt of food stamps for either race. For whites only, there was a drop in income adequacy and socioeconomic status after retirement.

Thus, retirement reduced income and income adequacy for whites, but for blacks retirement opened a source of secure income—SSI. It should be noted that although economic status was reduced, retirement had no differential impact on assets, on attitude toward standard of living (NLS), or on extent of worry about money (RHS).

Health. Although initially blacks and whites had similar health status, on the final wave the health status of blacks was poorer than that of whites. For whites of both samples, but only for NLS blacks, health of the retired was significantly poorer than health of the nonretired. For reasons discussed earlier we hesitate to attribute the poorer health to retirement.

Activities. On all activities but extent of contact with friends, there were differences between whites and blacks: the whites were more active. Retirement, however, had an impact on only one activity—for whites it reduced extent of activity in formal organizations.

Attitudes. With the exception of happiness about leisure activities, and personal happiness, blacks had a poorer level of satisfaction in the areas examined (see Table 9.5) than did whites.

Regression analyses indicated that only attitude to retirement (which was consistently affected only among whites) and attitude to health (which is congruent with poorer health status) were consistently affected by retirement among either whites or blacks. Partial exceptions included lower life satisfaction and lower satisfaction with activity level among retired whites.

Thus, although there were statistically significant race differences in certain attitudes, retirement caused few changes in attitudes within either race.

TABLE 9.6

RHS. For Selected Consequences Amount of Variance Explained (R^2) by (1) Initial Status; (2) All but Retirement Variable; (3) Retirement Variable; for Each Measure of Retirement, by Race

	(1) R^2 Initial Status	(2) R^2 All but Retirement Variable	(3) R^2 Retirement Variable		
			Subjective Dichotomous	Objective Dichotomous	Objective Continuous
Economic					
Income					
White (−)[a]	.16	.19	.04	.02	.05
Black (−)	.13	.19	—	—	.05
Income adequacy					
White (−)	.22	.34	.05	.03	.07
Black (0)	.23	.29	—	—	—
Socioeconomic factor					
White (−)	.54	.57	.02	.01	.03
Black (0)	.44	.47	—	—	.03
Health					
Health factor					
White (−)	.14	.17	.02	.01	.03
Black (0)	.07	.31	—	—	—

Activities				
Formal organization				
White (−)	.49	.53	.01	—	.01
Black (0)	.52	.59	—	—	—
Attitudes				
Life satisfaction				
White (−)	.24	.29	.01	—	.02
Black (0)	.11	.17	—	—	—
Attitude to retirement				
White (+)	NA[b]	.05	.07	.04	.05
Black (0)	NA	.19	.03	—	—

[a](+) Retirement related to better status.
(0) Retirement does not help explain status.
(−) Retirement related to poorer status.

[b]NA = Not available.

Retirement has no effect, or no consistent effect for the following:
Activities—solitary/sedentary; extent of contact with family; extent of contact with friends; extra-work interest.
Attitudes—attitude to work; satisfaction with activity; worry about finances.

TABLE 9.7

NLS. For Selected Consequences Amount of Variance Explained (R^2) by (1) Initial Status; (2) All but Retirement Variable; (3) Retirement Variable; for Each Measure of Retirement, by Race

	(1) R^2 Initial Status	(2) R^2 All but Retirement Variable	(3) R^2 Retirement Variable		
			Subjective Dichotomous	Objective Dichotomous	Objective Continuous
Economic					
Family income					
White (−)[a]	.16	.20	.01	.01	.02
Black (−)	.15	.17	—	.02	.02
Receipt of SSI					
White (0)	NA[b]	.05	—	—	—
Black (+)	NA	.19	.04	.02	.04

Health					
Health limitation					
White (-)	.09	.21	.04	.04	.05
Black(-)	.03	.12	.07	.04	.12
Combined health items					
White (-)	NA	.19	.04	.03	.04
Black (-)	NA	.15	.06	.05	.07
Health (happiness with)					
White (-)	NA	.17	.07	.03	.05
Black (-)	NA	.13	.05	.04	.05

[a](-) Retirement related to poorer status.
(0) Retirement does not help explain status.
(+) Retirement related to receipt of SSI.

[b] NA = Not available.

Retirement has no effect, or no consistent effect for the following:
Economic—assets; food stamps.
Attitudes—extent of happiness with house; area of residence; leisure activities; and personal happiness.

DISCUSSION

Unlike the majority of studies which have compared black males with white males, the present study is longitudinal. Further, it examines two samples. The former procedure permits us to determine what happens to a particular cohort over time controlling for initial characteristics; the latter permits us to determine the generalizability of our findings.

The samples we used were nationally representative and the comparative demographic, occupational, and economic standings of the blacks and whites were as expected: in both studies blacks were in a poorer position than whites. Baseline health status, however, was equivalent for both groups.

It is important to note that, although the position of blacks was poorer, the variances in the measures used were comparable to those of whites. In addition, the sample sizes were substantial. Some findings from blacks were checked by reanalyzing the data using a sample three times the original size. The findings were always upheld. It is unlikely that statistical artifact can account for the findings reported here.

Predicting Retirement

While several categories were important in predicting retirement for whites, only a minimum number was important for blacks. This finding held for both data sets, and within data sets for each of the three definitions of retirement, even though these definitions had been operationalized slightly differently in the two data sets. Such consistency supports the validity and reliability of these findings. For whites retirement can best be predicted by a combination of information from all five areas (demographic, socioeconomic, health, job characteristics, and attitudes) with each area generally represented by several significant variables. For blacks few areas are important, and those few are rarely represented by more than one variable.

These data suggest that only the most crucial matters determining the possibility of working or the feasibility of retirement are important for blacks (age, health, education, job stability); whereas for whites, retirement is influenced by a much more complicated range of matters.

The findings support our hypothesis that for blacks, a restricted set of characteristics is important for predicting retirement. This is probably attributable to their poorer educational opportunities when young, their consequent ineligibility for many types of work, and job discrimination through most of their working lives. Under such restricted circumstances there is little opportunity for a broad array of factors to influence their retirement. Nor is there much reason for most blacks to have much personal investment in their work. Work is less rewarding for most blacks, as seen by the reduced likelihood of a second pension and lower social security retirement benefits. White males were always in a better position to match their jobs to their skills and inclinations. We find, for instance, that the correlation among education, occupational status, and income adequacy is higher for white males than for black males. Work for whites more closely reflects their unique characteristics, and this is evidenced by the importance of a broader array of categories when predicting cessation or reduction of work, i.e., retirement.

Consequences of Retirement

Carrying the same argument further we would expect retirement to have less impact on blacks than on whites because of blacks' lesser investment and involvement in work.

Our data indicate that the impact of retirement is most noticeable in the economic area, and on attitude to retirement. Retirement has little consistent explanatory power for the many other activities and attitudes examined here.

In those areas where retirement does appear to be influential, the impact of retirement varies by race and by data set, having a lesser impact for blacks than for whites on one data set (RHS) but a greater impact on the other (NLS). This discrepancy is probably related to the differences in time intervals and samples. RHS spans 6 years, while NLS spans 10 years. Since participants had the same age range on the final wave examined (they were then 64 to 69 years old), the NLS participants included workers four years younger than the youngest RHS workers. A great deal happens during those four years. In particular the less healthy, and a disproportionate number of blacks, retire (Daymont, 1981; Schwab, 1976). Over half of those no longer in the RHS labor force sample retired within the previous four years (Schwab, 1976). All of these people are represented in the NLS sample.

This means that NLS included many blacks and persons with deteriorating health who were not represented in the RHS. Thus, compared to NLS, RHS represents older, more fortunate working males, especially among the blacks.

These differences in the samples may well explain why, where health is concerned, retirement has greater explanatory power for NLS than for RHS, and why the race effects are contrary in the two studies. A larger proportion of respondents in NLS, particularly black respondents, had deteriorating health. The NLS data reflect changes in health over a 10-year period, during the first 4 of which the main reason for retirement was poor health. RHS data reflect the last 6 years of this 10-year period, when alternative reasons for retirement became more prevalent. Although we have been discussing the relative amount of variance in health status explained by the retirement measures, we should remember that retirement probably does not cause the poor health. Here there is evidence that the poorer health usually occurs before retirement.

In the economic area different but complementary variables were explored in the two data sets. The findings are consistent. For both blacks and whites retirement results in a reduction in family income. This reduction is sufficiently large for whites that the adequacy of their income is significantly reduced and their socioeconomic status declines (RHS). However, these declines are not so substantial that they lead to more concern about money. This may be because certain expenses are reduced in retirement and this is not adequately reflected in our measure of income adequacy, i.e., income may be more adequate than our measure indicates. Income adequacy was not reduced among blacks (RHS), but retired blacks were more likely to receive SSI (NLS). Neither assets nor receipt of food stamps was affected by retirement. It should be recalled that eligibility for food stamps is only income-dependent, while eligibility for receipt of SSI is dependent on both income and age. In sum, retirement has an impact on the economic status of whites, but not on the economic well-being of blacks. This should not be taken to imply that the economic well-being of blacks in retirement is adequate. It simply means that their economic status after retiring is comparable to what it would have been had they continued working. Since 15% of blacks receive SSI and even more are eligible (Hill, 1978) the economic status of many in this group cannot be considered satisfactory.

The only activity significantly affected by retirement (reduced organizational participation by whites) probably reflects straitened economic circumstances. The only attitude consistently affected is attitude to retirement (RHS), which is more likely to be positive among retired whites. The retirement attitude of blacks is not consistently affected. This is to be expected if, as hypothesized, work plays a less integral role in the lives of blacks than in the lives of whites.

Retirement has been assumed to have a very broad impact (Irelan, 1972). Our findings, on the contrary, show that the impact of retirement is usually quite limited. The most important effects are economic and on attitudes toward retirement. Even these limited effects appear mainly among whites. Blacks are rarely affected.

We believe that there are two main reasons for such lack of impact on blacks: the effects of discrimination in education and employment, and the receipt of transfer income after retirement.

Although some blacks of this generation have succeeded notably, the education and employment opportunities were not commensurate with the innate abilities of most blacks. Under such circumstances we should not expect work to have the extensive rewards described by Friedmann and Havighurst (1954); most rewards came from elsewhere. In such circumstances work demands less and rewards less, and therefore the cessation of work— retirement— has less impact.

We also believe that the introduction of SSI in 1974, which ensured uniform minimum incomes for the elderly, the marked improvements in social security benefits in 1969 and their later indexing, and the availability of Medicaid, have reduced the direct impact of retirement for the most disadvantaged group, the blacks.

The enforcement of antidiscriminatory employment policies have been shown to have had a salutory impact on the incomes and occupations of younger black men (Abbott, 1980) and possibly also for older black men (Daymont, 1981). If such enforcement is continued, if Social Security benefits and SSI are maintained, and as blacks with better education enter the labor force, we would expect the retirement experiences of blacks and whites to become more comparable. Such improvement, however, will be slow given the current economic and political conditions, with unemployment falling hardest on blacks and federal antidiscriminatory pressures weakening (Jencks, 1983). Differences between blacks and whites may be with us for a long time.

10
Differences among Socioeconomic Levels

In this chapter we examine whether the same or different factors predict retirement for persons at different socioeconomic levels, and whether the consequences of retirement are comparable regardless of socioeconomic level. There is reason to expect that different factors predict retirement for persons at different socioeconomic levels, and that the consequences of retirement differ also.

While it has long been maintained that many older persons enter poverty only after they retire, no studies appear to have been done which examine the predictors or impact of retirement on persons of different economic levels. There have been studies concerning income replacement rates (e.g., Fox, 1976; 1979; Schulz et al., 1974, 1980); attitudes to, knowledge about, and desire for preparation for retirement by persons of different occupational status (e.g., Fillenbaum & Maddox, 1974; Simpson & McKinney, 1966); and assessment of postretirement adjustment of blue-collar and white-collar workers (e.g., Stokes & Maddox, 1968). The majority of these studies focus on occupational status. However, while there is a general relationship between occupational status and income, there is also a considerable overlap in the earnings of different occupations. The low earnings of many teachers and ministers and the high earnings of many steel and automobile workers are standard examples of such overlap. Consequently it is inappropriate to make inferences regarding the determinants and consequences of retirement for persons at different economic levels from occupational status information.

An earlier version of this chapter will appear in the *Journal of Gerontology*. Used by permission.

We first examine which factors determine retirement for three socioeconomic levels: the working poor, those with marginal incomes, and the more affluent. In the chapter on "Predictors of Retirement" we suggested that there were five groups of important predictors of retirement: demographic characteristics, socioeconomic status, health, job characteristics, and attitudes toward work and retirement. These predictors were viewed as a causal chain, each area having both direct effects on retirement and indirect effects through subsequent areas. The analysis of three national and four local longitudinal studies supported this hypothesis.

The relevance and importance of these areas, however, may be different at different economic levels. For the working poor it is hard to hypothesize which areas, if any, are important. Demographic characteristics and health would seem to be the main influences. Of the demographic characteristics, age is probably the most important but its relationship is probably curvilinear. We would expect some persons to retire at the earliest age feasible so that they could be assured of some steady income, which might differ little from what they make when working, while for others the difference between work and retirement income might be a strong inducement to continue to work as long as possible. Health is probably decisive. We expect that those working poor who retire would be more likely to be in poor health. We expect that there is so little variation in socioeconomic status or job characteristics (as measured in the available longitudinal studies) that on statistical grounds alone these should not be important predictors. In addition, the working poor may not have the luxury of letting their attitudes to work and retirement determine their future actions.

At the marginal and upper income levels we expect all five areas to be important since greater variance (in the indicators of socioeconomic status and job characteristics) should be present; but we do not expect to find substantial differences in the predictors of retirement between the marginal and upper income workers.

If retirement does indeed propel certain people into poverty, then the consequences of retirement should be different for each of the three groups. We have classified the diverse consequences of retirement into four categories: income, health, activities, and attitudes. Each will be considered in turn as to its hypothesized relationship to the economic level of workers.

Income. Because of age-related income supports we expected that the working poor would be no worse off economically after retirement than they were before retirement. In fact, they could be better off, because Supplemental Security Income payments become available at age 65. Comparable income transfer payments are not available below this age. For both marginal and upper level groups, we expected a decline in economic adequacy. This decline was expected to be greater for the marginal economic level group, since the upper economic level retirees are more likely to receive second pensions, and to have accumulated greater assets.

Health. The effects of retirement on health are still unclear. As shown earlier, even when initial health status was controlled, reported health status was poorer among the retired than among the nonretired. However, the poorer later health could have developed during the period after the initial assessment but before retirement.

We expected differences among the economic levels in the relationship of retirement to health. Because the working poor are under less stress to find work or to continue working after retirement, we expected the least relationship of retirement to health among the working poor. We expected that there would be a relationship between retirement and health at the other two economic levels, and that this relationship would be similar at the two levels.

Activities. Among the working poor, we expected that retirement would not affect participation in activities, since most of their activities are not dependent on much income, and income was expected to change little after retirement. For the marginal and upper economic levels, we expected that only those activities which depend on money would be affected. We expected the impact of retirement on activities to be greater for the marginal group because of a greater decline in income or in income adequacy.

Attitudes. We did not expect attitudes to be affected by retirement, at least not to an extent observable by the measures available, unless those attitudes referred specifically to retirement. Among the poor we did not expect even attitudes to retirement to be affected by retirement, but among the marginal and upper level groups we expected the retired to develop a more positive view of retirement, because they have coped with the anxieties and problems of retirement more than the nonretirees. We did not expect retirement to have a differential effect on the attitudes of marginal and upper level groups.

DATA SOURCES

Of the seven longitudinal studies considered, only the Social Security Administration's Retirement History Study (RHS) and the National Longitudinal Surveys (NLS) provided samples of adequate size and contained sufficient information on income to permit accurate division of their samples into the three economic levels: the working poor, marginal, and upper level.

ECONOMIC LEVELS

Economic level was defined not in terms of income alone, but in terms of income adequacy (income in relation to standards for families of different size) at baseline. The working poor were persons whose income was no greater than the Federal poverty standard; those in a marginal position had incomes above the poverty level but no greater than the Federal intermediate budget level; those at the upper level had incomes higher than the Federal intermediate budget level.

MEASURES OF RETIREMENT

For each data set three measures of retirement were developed: a subjective dichotomous measure, an objective dichotomous measure, and an objective continuous measure indicating extent of continued participation in the labor force. The specific manner in which these were operationalized was described earlier. Because the information available differed somewhat in the two data sets, the measures of retirement are only approximately equivalent across data sets.

SAMPLES

In order to examine the determinants and consequences of retirement by economic levels, only men who were not retired at the start of the study and who were active members of the labor force (working at least 16 hours a week) were included. To facilitate comparisons across studies only those who would be aged 64 to 69 on the final wave examined were selected. The time intervals and dates of the initial and final waves varied from study to study, as shown below:

Study	Initial Age	Final Age	Interval	Time Span
RHS	58–63	64–69	6 years	1969–1975
NLS	54–59	64–69	10 years	1966–1976

ANALYSIS

Predictors of Retirement. Logistic regression was used in examining predictors of retirement when retirement was dichotomously defined. Ordinary least squares (OLS) multiple regression was used to examine predictors of the continuous retirement measure (participation in the labor force).

Consequences of Retirement. OLS multiple regression was used in examining the consequences of retirement. Some consequences were measured dichotomously (e.g., receipt of food stamps); however, since previous analyses had shown that OLS regression yielded results similar to that obtained from logistic regression, the former was used throughout to facilitate comparisons among consequences.

CHARACTERISTICS OF THE SAMPLES

Basic information permitting comparison of low, marginal, and upper economic level persons in each study is given in Table 10.1. The relative proportions of persons at each of the three levels and the proportions of blacks differs across studies, reflecting the sampling techniques used (RHS: random sample; NLS: oversampling of blacks). Within each study the ages of the three economic groups are comparable. Across studies the ages reflect the sample ages.

As economic level improves, amount of education and occupational status increase. The sole exception is the "low" group for RHS, whose higher occupational status reflects an unusually high

TABLE 10.1
Basic Characteristics of the Samples

	RHS Economic Level			NLS Economic Level		
	Low	Marginal	High	Low	Marginal	High
N	86	395	987	95	243	641
Age						
Mean	60.40	60.11	60.18	56.18	56.37	56.33
S.D.	1.77	1.66	1.70	1.70	1.67	1.70
Race						
% Black[a]	17	15	4	67	40	5
Socioeconomic						
Education						
Mean	7.95	8.60	10.94	5.16	7.12	10.59
S.D.	3.36	3.36	3.39	3.43	3.25	3.64
Occupational status						
Mean	5.70	4.62	5.83	13.78	19.50	40.78
S.D.	2.32	2.14	2.22	12.35	14.97	25.08
Marital status						
% Married	90	92	90	83	86	90
Health						
Mean	3.56	3.35	2.66	2.65	2.99	3.28
S.D.	3.12	2.97	2.54	.95	.84	.73
% Retired:						
Dichotomous definitions						
Subjective	79	82	79	60	66	64
Objective	76	74	74	83	84	79

[a]Only blacks and whites are included in these samples. Other races have been excluded because of their small numbers.

rate of self-employment (52%) and hence higher occupation classification as an "owner." Marital status is similar across economic
levels and studies. Finally, health is positively related to economic
level.

Within each study the proportion retired is similar across economic levels. There are, however, noticeable differences in rate of
retirement across studies, reflecting the effect of slightly different
definitions of retirement.

RESULTS

Predictors of Retirement

Data were analyzed separately for each economic level within each
data set. We included in the final analyses only those variables
which were theoretically relevant and, for the economic level in
question, were significantly related to retirement. When there
was more than one such variable, the variables were grouped into
categories. These categories were ordered according to our model
(i.e., demographic, socioeconomic, health, job characteristics,
attitudes) and the categories entered stagewise. This permits
determination of the explanatory power added by each of the
succeeding categories.

We had hypothesized that only health would be important in
predicting the retirement of the working poor, but that all five
categories would be important predictors of retirement for the
other two economic levels. The data only partially supported our
expectations (Table 10.2). For RHS and NLS the number of different categories which made a significant contribution in predicting retirement increased with increase in economic level. However, the specific categories were sometimes not those expected.
For low economic level RHS men, health (for subjectively defined
retirement), job characteristics (for the objective dichotomous
definition) and both health and job characteristics (for continued
participation in the labor force) were important. In the NLS low
level, only job characteristics were ever important.

For RHS men at the marginal level, two categories were consistently important, regardless of how retirement was defined:
demographic and job characteristics. In addition, health was important for the subjective definition, socioeconomic status for the
objective dichotomous definition, and health again for the labor

TABLE 10.2

Significant Predictors of Retirement, by Category, for Three
Economic Levels, and Three Measures of Retirement by Data Set

	RHS Economic Level			NLS Economic Level		
	Low	Marginal	High	Low	Marginal	High
Subjective Dichotomous Definition of Retirement						
Demographic		+a	+			+
Socioeconomic			+			+
Health	+	+	+		+	
Job characteristics		+	+	+	+	+
Attitudes			+			+
Total R	.15	.31	.44	.17	.23	.32
Objective Dichotomous Definition of Retirement						
Demographic		+	+			+
Socioeconomic		+	+			+
Health			+			
Job characteristics	+	+	+		+	+
Attitudes			+			+
Total R	.21	.39	.49		.30	.37
Objective Continuous Definition of Retirement						
Demographic		+	+		+	+
Socioeconomic			+			+
Health	+	+	+		+	
Job characteristics	+	+	+	+	+	+
Attitudes			+			+
Total R^2	.21	.16	.24	.09	.18	.18

a+ Category is significant predictor of retirement.

force definition. Findings from NLS were similar, although fewer areas were significant. Here job characteristics were also consistently important. In addition, health was important for the subjective assessment of retirement, and both health and demographic variables for the labor force definition.

Among men at the upper economic level all areas were important for RHS and all but health were important for NLS. The latter result was probably due to the limited measure of health available for NLS.

In addition to this consistency between RHS and NLS in number and type of areas important in predicting retirement at each economic level, there was also consistency in the extent to which retirement could be predicted. With rare exception, prediction improved as economic level increased. This probably reflects the greater diversity of areas significant as economic level improves.

Prediction tends to be more accurate for RHS than for NLS. This probably reflects the shorter time span between initial assessment and final wave examined in RHS (6 years as compared with 10 years in NLS).

Consequences of Retirement

As before, the consequences examined were arranged into four categories: economic, health, activities, and attitudes. The specific items examined within each category depended on the information available within each data set, and are listed below.

	RHS	NLS

Economic	(B)[a] Family income
	(B) Income adequacy
	(B) Socioeconomic functioning
		(B) Family income
		(B) Poverty ratio
		      SSI receipt
		      Food stamps receipt
		(B) Assets

Health	(B) Health	(B) Health limitation Sum of three health items
Activities	(B) Formal organizations (B) Extra-work interests Extent of contact w/: (B) Family (B) Friends (B) Solitary/sedentary activities	

Attitudes	(B) Life satisfaction
	      Attitude to retirement
	      Attitude to work
	      Satisfaction with
	        activity level
	      Worry about finances
		Happiness with:
		  Housing
		  Local residential area
		  Health condition
		  Standard of living
		  Leisure time activities
		Self-rated happiness

[a]*(B) = Baseline data available*

Analysis of each consequence was by means of OLS multiple regression. First to enter was baseline status on the consequence (when baseline data were available), then all other statistically significant baseline variables, and finally the measure of retirement. Regressions were run separately for each of the three economic levels, and for each of the three measures of retirement. Such replication permitted us to determine whether a particular consequence was related to retirement in general or just to a specific definition of retirement.

Tables 10.3 and 10.4 present information on the amount of variance explained (R^2) at each relevant step of the analysis for each consequence and measure of retirement.

Economic. Family income on the last wave was examined in both RHS and NLS. In the NLS retirement does not help to explain final wave income for the working poor at all. But retirement does cause a decline in income among the marginal and upper levels. On RHS the impact of retirement is similar for these levels, but in NLS the main impact of retirement falls on the marginal level. This finding suggests that, as posited, income replacement may be more feasible for persons at the upper than for persons at the marginal level, and that retirement has little impact on income at the lowest level. On RHS only extent of labor force participation helped explain later income for the working poor (those who worked more had a higher income).

Income is important, but income does not take into account the number of persons for whom that income must provide. Of greater relevance than income is the adequacy of that income: how well it provides for sustenance, shelter, clothing and care, and permits unashamed participation in society (Townsend, 1979). Standards of income adequacy were available for each of the three data sets.

The analysis of income adequacy indicates that retirement does not change income adequacy for those at the lowest level. While NLS data indicate that retirement has no impact at the marginal and upper levels either, RHS data suggest that retirement results in a decline in income adequacy at these levels.

Detailed examination of income adequacy (Table 10.5) indicates that between the initial and final waves of the studies examined, the adequacy of income of the working poor increased markedly (for both retired and nonretired), indeed in RHS it became comparable to that of the marginal group; the income adequacy of the marginal group remained stable; while that of the

TABLE 10.3
Significant Consequences of Retirement by Economic Level among RHS Men

	(1) R^2 Initial Status	(2) R^2 All but Retirement Variable	(3) R^2 Retirement Variable		
			Objective Dichotomous	Objective Continuous	Subjective Dichotomous
Economic					
Income					
EL[a]: Low (-)[b]	.01	.24	—	.05	—
Marginal (-)	.11	.15	—	.05	.04
High (-)	.13	.16	.03	.06	.04
Income adequacy					
EL: Low (-)	.37	.42	—	—	—
Marginal (-)	.11	.16	.02	.07	.06
High (-)	.15	.25	.04	.08	.05
Socioeconomic level					
EL: Low (-)	.53	.58	—	—	—
Marginal (-)	.48	.51	.01	.03	.02
High (-)	.47	.51	.02	.04	.03
Health					
Health					
EL: Low (-)	.14	.20	—	—	—
Marginal (-)	.16	.20	—	.04	.02
High (-)	.11	.14	.01	.04	.03
Activities					
Formal organizations					
EL: Low (-)	.35	.45	—	.06	—
Marginal (-)	.47	.54	—	.01	—
High (-)	.48	.52	—	.01	.01

Extra-work interests					
EL: Low	.56	.59	—	—	—
Marginal	.50	.54	—	—	—
High (+)	.51	.52	.01	.01	.01
Personal work control					
EL: Low (−)	.24	.26	.06	.43	.16
Marginal (−)	.07	.12	.07	.51	.30
High (−)	.04	.12	.24	.47	.50
Attitudes					
Life satisfaction					
EL: Low	.25	.36	—	—	—
Marginal (−)	.11	.18	—	.05	.02
High (−)	.22	.28	—	.01	—
Attitude to retirement					
EL: Low	NA^c	.06	—	—	—
Marginal (+)	NA	.04	—	.03	.04
High (+)	NA	.06	.06	.06	.09
Satisfaction with activity level					
EL: Low	NA	.06	—	—	—
Marginal (−)	NA	.09	—	.02	—
High (−)	NA	.09	—	.01	.01
Worry about finances					
EL: Low	NA	.05	—	—	—
Marginal (+)	NA	.08	.02	.04	.04
High	NA	.09	—	—	—

Consequences tested but found not significant for any of the three economic levels were: Frequency of contact with nonresident family; frequency of contact with friends; participation in solitary or sedentary activities; and attitude to work.

^a EL = Economic level.

^b (−) Decrease or negative effect among the retired.
(+) Increase or positive effect among the retired.

^c NA = Not available.

TABLE 10.4
Significant Consequences of Retirement by Economic Level among NLS Men

	(1) R^2 Initial Status	(2) R^2 All but Retirement Variable	(3) R^2 Retirement Variable		
			Objective Dichotomous	Objective Continuous	Subjective Dichotomous
Economic					
Family income, 1976					
EL[a]: Low	.21	.21	—	—	—
Marginal (−)[b]	—	—	.02	.05	.02
High (−)	.14	.17	.01	.01	—
Poverty ratio, 1976					
EL: Low (−)	.03	.03	—	—	—
Marginal (−)	.14	.14	—	—	—
High (−)	.37	.51	—	—	—
Receipt of SSI					
EL: Low (+)	NA[c]	.14	—	.11	.09
Marginal (+)	NA	.07	.02	.01	.01
High	NA	.00	—	—	—
Receipt of food stamps					
EL: Low (+)	NA	—	.08	.16	.12
Marginal (+)	NA	.10	.01	.01	.03
High	NA	.00	—	—	—
Assets, 1976					
EL: Low (−)	.67	—	—	—	—
Marginal (−)	.26	.26	.01	.03	.02
High	.15	.27	—	—	—

		Col A	Col B	Col C	Col D	Col E
Health						
Health limitations						
EL:	Low (−)	—	—	.17	.25	.21
	Marginal (−)	.05	.05	.08	.10	.06
	High (−)	.06	.12	.06	.06	.05
Health combination						
EL:	Low (−)	NA	—	.07	.15	.13
	Marginal (−)	NA	.05	.05	.06	.09
	High (−)	NA	.16	.02	.01	.01
Happiness with:						
Health condition						
EL:	Low (−)	NA	—	—	.08	.09
	Marginal (−)	NA	.06	.04	.04	.08
	High (−)	NA	.16	.02	.03	.02
Standard of living						
EL:	Low (−)	NA	—	—	—	—
	Marginal (−)	NA	—	—	.02	.02
	High	NA	.06	—	—	—
Leisure time activities						
EL:	Low (−)	NA	—	—	—	—
	Marginal (−)	NA	—	—	—	.01
	High (−)	NA	.05	.01	—	—
Self-rated happiness						
EL:	Low (−)	NA	—	—	—	—
	Marginal (−)	NA	—	—	.02	.02
	High	NA	.09	—	—	—

Consequences tested but found not significant for any of the three economic levels were attitude to personal housing and to local area of residence.

aEL = Economic level.

b(−) Decrease or negative effect among the retired.
(+) Increase or positive effect among the retired.

cNA = Not available.

TABLE 10.5
Income and Income Adequacy by Economic Level and Final Wave Retirement Status, Objectively Assessed, for RHS and NLS

	Low Economic Level Ret. Status on Final Wave		Marginal Economic Level Ret. Status on Final Wave		High Economic Level Ret. Status on Final Wave	
	Not ret.	Retired	Not ret.	Retired	Not ret.	Retired
RHS N	20	63	93	276	253	731
Income R + Spouse, 1969						
Mean	1494	1338	5208	5109	13107	11523
S.D.	1368	1051	2041	1992	8540	5828
Income R + Spouse, 1975						
Mean	4084	5635	5254	4502	12843	7620
S.D.	4962	7881	5043	3818	16285	7759
Income adequacy, 1969						
Mean	1.00	1.00	2.98	2.95	5.39	5.34
S.D.	.00	.00	.88	.86	.49	.47
Income adequacy, 1975						
Mean	3.00	3.21	3.36	2.88	5.05	4.20
S.D.	1.45	1.51	1.39	1.15	1.15	1.30
NLS N	16	73	37	188	137	504
Family income, 1966						
Mean	1973	1771	4710	4940	16256	11311
S.D.	1279	1017	1977	1966	14241	6508
Family income, 1976						
Mean	4369	4179	6796	4772	14566	8770
S.D.	3648	6816	6492	4651	19400	9630
Poverty ratio, 1966						
Mean	.63	.62	1.82	1.89	7.46	5.00
S.D.	.23	.25	.46	.49	8.10	2.70
Poverty ratio, 1976						
Mean	1.59	1.15	2.38	2.46	6.12	4.50
S.D.	1.43	.84	1.34	1.71	4.82	2.59

upper group declined somewhat, but was still greater than for the marginal group. The stability of income adequacy in the marginal group at a time when their income was decreasing was probably due to a reduction in the number of dependents. Among the working poor, RHS and NLS data indicate that increase in income adequacy was due to a substantial increase in monetary income. The data suggest a leveling effect—the well-off are no longer so well off (but nevertheless maintain their relative position) while there has been a marked improvement in the condition of the poor.

Among the other economic variables examined are a factor analytically derived measure of socioeconomic status (RHS), and receipt of SSI, food stamps, and assets (NLS). The results indicate that retirement does cause a decline in socioeconomic status among retired middle and upper level men (RHS) and reduced assets among middle level men (NLS). Retirement had no significant effects regarding assets for the poorest, perhaps because they had too little to be affected, or among the better off, who may not have needed to use their savings. On the other hand retirement was positively related to receipt of SSI and food stamps, particularly among the poor (R^2 ranging from .04 to .11 for SSI and .08 to .12 for food stamps) and less so among those at the marginal level (R^2 ranging from .01 to .03). Few at the marginal and upper levels received these forms of support.

Health. We had predicted that the better the economic level the greater would be the reported decline of health among the retired. This prediction was borne out for RHS, but just the reverse was found for NLS. In NLS retirement was related to poorer health, but the explanatory power of retirement was inversely related to economic level.

Activities. The various activities examined were little affected by retirement for any economic level. At the upper economic level there was some decrease in participation in formal organizations, and greater involvement in extra-work interests. Regardless of economic level retirement was not related to frequency of contact with family and friends, or to pursuit of solitary or sedentary activities.

Attitudes. Regardless of economic level, retirement had little impact on attitudes. The primary exception was attitude to retirement (RHS). Positive attitudes to retirement resulted from the experience of retirement, the effect being greater for upper than for marginal economic level men—and absent for the poor. Worrying about finances (RHS) was greater among the retired, but only at the marginal economic level. Life satisfaction was decreased in the marginal group also, but the finding was not consistent across all three measures of retirement. Attitude to work and satisfaction with activity level were barely affected, if at all. In the NLS the most notable negative impact of retirement on attitudes was with respect to health (which was discussed earlier). Retirement was also related to reduced happiness and to lesser satisfaction with standard of living among the marginal economic level retired. Neither lower nor upper economic level persons were affected. This probably reflects the poorer economic position of the marginal income retired vis-à-vis the nonretired.

DISCUSSION

Although members of the three economic levels retired at similar rates, the factors determining their retirement differed noticeably. Among the poorest only the most basic matters were important—whether their health permitted them to work, and whether they could get a job. Among those at the marginal level the availability of a job, compulsory retirement, and the availability of a pension were important. For this group the availability of work and the rewards of working, i.e., a pension, were important in determining retirement. But other matters also had relevance: age, health, marital status, number of persons in the household. Thus, more of the individual's personal life and life history were involved at this level. Finally, with the upper economic level there was the broadest involvement, so that all of the main areas were implicated: demographic, socioeconomic, health, job characteristics, and attitudes regarding work or retirement. Thus, as economic level improved more areas affected retirement. These findings seem to indicate that for upper level persons various aspects of life are more interdependent than they are for lower level persons.

Retirement was expected to have an impact on diverse areas of functioning. However, these results show that the impact of retirement is most noticeable where economic and health matters are concerned, but has little impact on most activities or attitudes.

The financial impact of retirement varied by economic level, and was most noticeable for those at the marginal level. In RHS and NLS retirement caused a consistent, if small, reduction in income for marginal level persons. Also for marginal level persons retirement reduced assets, the adequacy of income (RHS only), and general socioeconomic level. Retirement tended to be of less importance at the upper level, where it did reduce income adequacy and socioeconomic level but was otherwise inconsequential. Retirement's only economic effect for low income men was an increase in receipt of SSI and food stamps.

The marked improvement in income, and the adequacy of income of the working poor after retirement, not only confirms Coe's (1978) findings that families may move in and out of poverty, but for this particular cohort suggests that the substantial improvements in Social Security which started in 1969, and the introduction of SSI in January 1974, have resulted in an impressive improvement in the financial status of the poorest group when they enter the retirement years. Unlike the marginal and upper levels, the income of the poorest improved, and the purchasing power of that income improved also, for they used subsidies such as food stamps. While there was a sharp decline in the income adequacy of the upper level group, their general economic position remained adequate. The marginal economic level retained its financial status relative to the other levels, but retirement for this group diminished assets, increased worry about their financial circumstances, reduced satisfaction with their standard of living, and diminished personal happiness.

So while the poorest benefited over these years and from retirement, and the upper group experienced the greatest economic decline, it was the marginal group which was most concerned about its economic status. Psychologically they may indeed be in the most precarious position, for on the final wave the adequacy of their income was comparable to that of the poorest group, and their assets were diminished. Where the poor have improved their status, the marginal level has declined, and while the upper level retired men have also experienced a drop relative to their initial position, they usually have a financial cushion that can absorb such a drop. At the upper level, retirement did not result in greater worry about finances, as it did for the marginal level group.

At all three levels, retirement is related to poorer health. For each level this relationship is much more marked for NLS than for RHS. Further, while the explanatory value of retirement was inversely related to economic level for NLS (i.e., the lower the economic level the higher the R^2), the reverse was found for RHS. This difference seems puzzling. Since the measures of health on RHS and NLS were comparable it seems unlikely that these explain the differences found. They are probably attributable to differences in sampling (NLS oversampled blacks by a factor of approximately three) and in the time interval covered (10 years in NLS, 6 years in RHS) and consequently in the younger initial age of the NLS males. Schwab (1976) studied those RHS men who, on the initial wave, were no longer members of the labor force. She found that a disproportionate number of nonparticipants were in poor health (and were nonparticipants for this reason), had been in manual occupations which were typically lower paying, and were black. The majority of these persons had still been in the labor force four years earlier. Consequently, included in the NLS sample are persons who have already dropped out of the RHS sample. Further, we are seeing them in exaggerated numbers because of the NLS oversampling of blacks. Thus Schwab's (1976) findings may explain why retirement better explains health in NLS than in RHS—NLS contains more people who are likely to retire because of ill health. Although the method of analysis attributes the ill health to retirement, Schwab's findings indicate that incapacity usually occurred before retirement.

Schwab's findings also help to explain why, in RHS, retirement better explains poor health among upper economic level retirees while in NLS the situation is reversed. In all likelihood this is due to differential dropout of the health impaired, with dropout being greater as economic level declines. Such dropout could result in the RHS findings.

Thus, although the health findings on NLS and RHS seemed to be contradictory, there does seem to be a reasonable explanation which reconciles the findings. Longer term follow-up of middle-aged workers indicates that the retired are likely to be in poorer health than the nonretired, the difference being particularly marked as economic level declines. Shorter term follow-up of older workers, a more select group, suggests that health, as an explanation of retirement, increases in importance as economic level improves.

Regardless of economic level, retirement seems to have little consistent effect, if any, on activities. Upper level men may participate somewhat less in formal organizations and have somewhat more extra-work interests after retirement but such change is minor. Neither are attitudes much affected, aside from attitude to retirement, to which the upper level retired are more positively inclined. This minimal impact of retirement indicates that retirement usually does not become a disruptive force and most aspects of life can be continued as before.

These results show that our initial fears regarding the impact of retirement were largely groundless. The working poor were not constrained to direst poverty, the income of the more affluent dropped somewhat, but the adequacy of their income remained fairly stable and they did not show increased concern about their financial position. It was the marginal group which was most affected. While their relative economic level remained secure, their savings dropped and financial matters were of distinct concern. Nevertheless the changes which did occur resulted in few differences in activities or attitudes.

11
Summary and Implications

Our research on the antecedents and consequences of retirement was designed to overcome several weaknesses of previous research by: (1) being based on longitudinal data (which permits control for initial status); (2) being based on three nationally representative samples and four representative local samples; (3) using multivariate statistical techniques (which permits simultaneous control for all relevant variables); (4) comparing change over time among those who retire with those who do not; (5) comparing results from three different definitions of retirement; (6) comparing differences in retirement among policy relevant subgroups: men and women, blacks and whites, upper and lower SES groups, early and on-time retirees, voluntary and involuntary retirees, the fully retired and those who return to work.

We will summarize our findings from each chapter with a series of propositions followed by our theoretical interpretations and a discussion of the implications. It should be understood that our statements of policy implications are only our opinions, based on our values and assumptions. Others may well reach differing opinions based on other values and assumptions. We will close with a discussion of promising directions for future research.

PREDICTION OF RETIREMENT

1. The strongest predictors of dichotomously defined retirement are structural factors such as SES and job characteristics. Health and attitudes are relatively poor predictors.
2. The strongest predictors of continuously defined retirement are job characteristics, which are more important than all other predictors added together.

166

3. Subjective variables such as health and attitude are strong predictors of early retirement, but structural factors are equally important.

Interpretation. Most retirement at normal ages is forced or encouraged by mandatory retirement policies and expectations of employers, fellow workers, and family. Those who are self-employed or are not subject to mandatory retirement are most likely to continue to work full-time. In contrast, most early retirement is neither forced nor expected and is more influenced by subjective perceptions of health, work, and attractiveness of retirement benefits.

Implications. If reducing early retirement is a desired goal (to reduce the drain on the Social Security system and pension funds), then the most effective policies would focus on maintaining workers' health, making their work more attractive, and reducing the attractiveness of early retirement benefits. If delaying retirement beyond the normal retirement age is a desired goal, then the most effective policies would focus on eliminating mandatory retirement, discrimination against older workers, and reducing pressures for retirement (subtle and overt) from employers and fellow workers. Increasing opportunities for self-employment and part-time employment among older workers would also delay full retirement. Finally, delaying the availability of retirement benefits would have a strong effect on delaying retirement.

CONSEQUENCES OF RETIREMENT

4. Controlling for preretirement characteristics and the effects of aging reduces the income drop so that the average retiree retains about three-fourths of preretirement income. This contrasts with earlier research which concludes that retirement income is only one-half of preretirement income.

5. Retirement at the normal age has little or no adverse effects on health for the average retiree. Some have health declines, but these are balanced by those who enjoy health improvement.

6. Retirement at the normal age has few substantial effects on activities, except for the obvious reduction in work and some compensating increase in solitary activities.

7. Retirement at the normal age has little or no effect on most attitudes for the average retiree. Some become more dissatisfied, but these are balanced by those who become more satisfied.

8. Early retirement causes greater loss of income than normal age retirement, and early retirement causes significant decreases in life satisfaction for the average retiree.

Interpretation. The discrepancies between our findings (little or no effects from normal age retirement) and other studies (which found retirees to be substantially poorer, sicker, less active, and less satisfied) are due to the other studies' failure: (1) to control for preretirement characteristics (which requires longitudinal data), and (2) to use multivariate analysis in order to control for the related variables.

However, early retirees include many who are forced to retire early because of poor health, age discrimination, or other involuntary reasons. These involuntary retirees outweigh those who retire voluntarily and so the average early retirement produces more negative effects.

Implications. Since retirement at normal age is neither harmful nor beneficial to the average retiree, public policy should neither encourage nor discourage retirement as a general rule. Rather, it should be devoted to maximizing free choice and available options. However, since early involuntary retirement tends to have negative effects, public policy should focus on reducing the factors forcing early retirement (poor health, age discrimination, and poor employment opportunities).

DETERMINANTS OF ADJUSTMENT

9. The primary predictors of adjustment are similar for both retirees and nonretirees (better health, income, education, more activities, and being married).

10. However, social activities are more influential on life satisfaction for retirees than for nonretirees.

Interpretation. The finding that retirees are generally similar to nonretirees, in terms of the determinants of satisfaction, is congruent with findings no. 4-7 (little or no retirement effects). However, the greater importance of social activities for retirees' adjustment is due to their reduction in job-related social activities.

Implications. Efforts to improve adjustment among retirees should be generally similar to those for nonretirees: they should focus on maintaining health, income, and opportunities for education, social activities, and marriage (or remarriage). However, for retirees it is especially important to maintain or increase opportunities for social activities.

REASONS FOR RETIREMENT

11. Those retiring because of poor health were a relatively disadvantaged group before retirement; those retiring for other compulsory reasons were better off; and those retiring for voluntary reasons were the most fortunate.

12. Similarly, those retiring for poor health suffered the most negative consequences; those retiring for other compulsory reasons suffered less; and voluntary retirees enjoyed several positive effects.

Interpretation. The voluntary retirees were the most fortunate before retirement because their health was good enough to permit a voluntary choice and their jobs were less likely to be subject to mandatory retirement. They enjoyed more positive benefits from retirement because retirement is what they wanted and they had the resources to take advantage of the benefits of retirement. Those who retired for compulsory reasons other than health were less advantaged than voluntary retirees because their jobs were subject to mandatory retirement, but more advantaged than poor health retirees because of their better health and relatively good pensions. The poor health retirees were the most disadvantaged because they were forced to retire and had neither the health nor other resources to enjoy retirement.

Implications. Programs to reduce negative effects of retirement should concentrate on those retiring for poor health, because they are the most vulnerable and most negatively affected group.

WORK AFTER RETIREMENT

13. Between a quarter and a third of retired men and women returned to work.

14. Nearly half of the working retired men worked all year long, and almost as many worked full-time.

15. The majority of working retirees had a job with the same status as their preretirement job, but there were more downward shifts in status than upward shifts.

16. The following types of retirees were more likely to return to work: males, younger, farmers or other self-employed, lower SES, and those without pensions.

17. In comparison to baseline measures, those not yet retired were better off than the working retired, but the working retired were better off than the fully retired.

Interpretation. Substantial proportions of retirees return to work at least part-time because they need the income, enjoy their work, and/or want to be useful. Most working retired were able to work at jobs with at least the same status as their preretirement jobs because of the skills and experience they had built up during their careers. Men and younger retirees were more likely to return to work because of greater work commitment, need for income, and/or job opportunities. Farmers and other self-employed were more likely to return to work because they lacked retirement pensions and had greater employment opportunities. Those with lower socioeconomic status returned to work primarily because they needed the income. Working part-time after retirement allows a retiree to enjoy some of the benefits of both retirement (increased leisure) and of employment (income supplementation, health maintenance, and life satisfaction).

Implications. Since retirees with greater employment opportunities (men and self-employed) return to work more often, increasing job opportunities for women and those not self-employed would probably increase the amount of return to work. Increasing return to work would benefit retirees through increased income, health maintenance, and life satisfaction.

GENDER DIFFERENCES

18. Among men, retirement is predicted by a wide range of variables, but age is the only significant predictor among women.
19. Among men, retirement has small but significant effects (positive and negative) on a wide range of outcomes, but there are few significant effects among women.

Interpretation. The theoretical models and variables used in our analysis were largely oriented toward retirement among men. As a consequence, major factors that explain individual differences in retirement among women were not included.

Implications. New theoretical models oriented toward women's retirement need to be developed and tested. Specifically, marital status, family history, and work history need to be taken into account.

RACIAL DIFFERENCES

20. Among whites, retirement is predicted by a wide range of variables, but only a few variables are significant predictors among blacks (primarily age, health, and SES).

21. Among whites, retirement has small but significant effects on a wide range of outcomes, but there are fewer significant effects among blacks.

Interpretation. For blacks, only the most crucial matters determining the feasibility of working or retiring are important, whereas for whites, retirement is influenced by a more complicated range of matters. This is attributable to blacks' poorer education, restricted job opportunities, and employment discrimination which restricts their freedom of choice. Similarly, retirement has fewer effects on blacks because their work has been less rewarding.

Implications. Programs to increase freedom of choice in work and retirement should give special attention to blacks because their choice is more restricted. On the other hand, programs to minimize negative effects of retirement need not give special attention to blacks because they tend to experience fewer negative effects (since they were at lower levels before retirement). Blacks need programs to increase their work opportunities and rewards *before* retirement.

SOCIOECONOMIC DIFFERENCES

22. The higher the economic level, the greater the number of retirement predictors.

23. The main differences between economic levels in terms of retirement effects were in the financial area: for the working poor, income and income adequacy *improved* after retirement; for the marginal level retirees, income, income adequacy, assets, and satisfaction with standard of living all declined; for the upper level retirees, only income adequacy declined.

Interpretation. Among the working poor only the most basic matters are important in determining retirement; for the marginal level there is more choice involved in the retirement decision and therefore more factors come into play; the upper level group has the most choice and therefore the most factors that are relevant to their retirement decision. The income of the working poor increased after retirement because their earnings were low before retirement and various programs for the aged poor have improved their financial situation. The financial effects of retirement were most negative on the marginal level because they were rarely poor enough to benefit from such programs as SSI and food stamps, but were not affluent enough to have the financial cushion to absorb the effects of income loss after retirement.

Implications. Programs to increase freedom of choice in retirement should focus on the lower SES levels, because they tend to have the least freedom. New programs to maintain income adequacy should focus on the marginal level because they are the most vulnerable.

FUTURE RESEARCH NEEDED

Despite our attempts to provide comprehensive answers to questions of the antecedents and consequences of retirement, our analyses have raised many questions whose answers require further research.

One general problem with the data on preretirement characteristics is that these characteristics may have been measured a year or two before retirement. For fixed characteristics such as age, sex, and race, this is not a problem. But for changeable characteristics such as health, income, and attitudes, there may be substantial changes between the time the baseline measures are made and the time retirement actually takes place. Ideally, we need a study in which the preretirement measures are taken the day before retirement. This may not be feasible, but a research design in which the investigators are notified of impending retirement so they can schedule an interview a few days before retirement would solve several problematic questions such as: Does the residual decline in health between pre- and postretirement measures occur entirely (or mostly) *before* retirement, or does some of it occur *after* (and because of) retirement? Is the discrepancy between the frequency of poor health as the cited reason for retirement and the relative unimportance of poor health as a predictor of retirement due to a frequent decline in health between the time of preretirement interviews and actual retirement? Would retirement prove to be more consequential if we had baseline measures just before retirement?

The failure of our analyses to find many significant antecedents or consequences among women could be interpreted several ways: Perhaps it is because work and retirement are less important to women than to men (at least in this generation). Or perhaps our male-oriented models do not include the key predictors and outcomes of retirement for women. Or perhaps the samples of women were too small to produce many significant results. Or perhaps the omission of married women workers from our major studies distorts the findings. Future research focused on work and retirement among women is necessary to answer these questions.

A related question is the extent to which the wife's retirement is related to the husband's retirement (and vice versa). In order to thoroughly examine this issue, longitudinal data on the characteristics and retirement date of both husband and wife in a large number of representative married couples is necessary. Ideally, such studies should use a cross-sequential design covering 10 years or more in order to examine period effects. As women become employed in more rewarding positions, the effect of husband's retirement on wife's retirement may decline.

Similarly, data on large numbers of never married, divorced and separated, and widowed persons are necessary to study the possible effects of these different nonmarried statuses. In our analysis, we combined all nonmarried persons into one category because we did not have large enough numbers to analyze the subcategories separately.

In the RHS and the NLS we have enough blacks to analyze separately, but we did not have enough of the other minority groups (Hispanic, Asiatic, Indian, etc.) to analyze separately. There are several reasons for expecting that work and retirement patterns are substantially different among each of these minority groups. However, there are no longitudinal data on large enough samples of these groups to permit examination of these different patterns.

It appears that retirees who return to work are better off after retirement than those who do not. Obviously, return to work increases income. But does it have other benefits such as maintenance of health and life satisfaction? Only a controlled experiment in which a randomly selected (rather than self-selected) group is induced to return to work and is compared to a control group who do not return to work can definitively answer this question.

If the data we had available had covered a longer time span, we could have done cross-sequential types of analysis to attempt the separation of age, period, and cohort effects (Palmore, 1978). As data from later waves become available, such analysis will become possible. We expect that there have been substantial period effects (related to fluctuations in the economy and new legislation against mandatory retirement), as well as possible cohort effects (related to better pension coverage and more pro-retirement attitudes among later cohorts). However, relatively long time spans and wide age ranges are necessary for such cross-sequential analysis of retirement. This should be an exciting development when it becomes possible.

These chapters have raised a number of other questions whose answers require further research. However, we believe that the present analysis has resulted in several important findings on the antecedents and consequences of retirement, with clear theoretical and policy relevance.

References

Abbott, J. Work experience and earnings of middle-aged black and white men, 1965-71. *Social Security Bulletin*, 1980, *43* (12), 16-34.

Anderson, J.A. Separate sample logistic discrimination. *Biometrika*, 1972, *59*, 19-35.

Ash, P. Pre-retirement counseling. *Gerontologist*, 1966, *6*, 97-99, 127-128.

Atchley, R. Retirement and leisure participation. Continuity or crisis? *Gerontologist*, 1971, *11*, 13-17. (a)

Atchley, R. Retirement and work orientation. *Gerontologist*, 1971, *11*, 29-32. (b)

Atchley, R. *The sociology of retirement.* New York. Schenkman, 1976.

Atchley, R. The process of retirement: The female experience. In M. Szinovacz (Ed.), *Women's retirement.* Beverly Hills, Ca.: Sage Publications, 1982.

Barfield, R.E., & Morgan, J.N. *Early retirement: The decision and the experience.* Ann Arbor, Mich.: Institute for Social Research, 1969.

Barfield, R., & Morgan, J. Trends in satisfaction with retirement. *The Gerontologist*, 1978, *18*, 19-23.

Bengtson, V. Differences between subsamples in level of present role activity. In R. Havighurst, B. Neugarten, J. Munnichs, & H. Thomae (Eds.), *Adjustment to retirement.* Netherlands: Van Gorkum, 1969.

Bixby, L., Kolodurbetz, W., Lauriat, P., & Murray, J. *Demographic and economic characteristics of the aged: 1968 social security survey.* Social Security Administration Office of Research and Statistics, Washington, D.C., 1975.

Bixby, L. Retirement patterns in the United States. *Social Security Bulletin*, 1976, *39*, 3-19.

Blinder, A.S., Gordon, R.H., & Wise, D.E. Reconsidering the work disincentive effects of social security. *National Tax Journal*, 1980, *33*, 431-442.

Block, M. Professional women: Work pattern as a correlate of retirement satisfaction. In M. Szinovacz (Ed.), *Women's retirement.* Beverly Hills, Ca.: Sage Publications, 1982.

Boskin, M.J. Social security and retirement decisions. *Economic Inquiry*, 1977, *15*, 1-25.

Bradburn, N. *The structure of psychological well-being.* Chicago: Aldine, 1969.

Burgess, E. Family structure and relationships. In E. Burgess (Ed.), *Aging in western societies*. Chicago: University of Chicago Press, 1960.

Burkhauser, R. The pension acceptance decision of older workers. *Journal of Political Economy*, 1979, *14*, 63-75.

Burkhauser, R.V., & Tolley, G.S. Older Americans and market work. *The Gerontologist*, 1978, *18*, 449-453.

Cantril, H. *The pattern of human concerns*. New Brunswick, N.J.: Rutgers University Press, 1965.

Carp, F. Differences among older workers, volunteers, and persons who are neither. *Journal of Gerontology*, 1968, *23*, 497-501.

Chow, G. Tests of equality between sets of coefficients in two linear regressions. *Econometrica*, 1960, *28*, 591-605.

Clague, E., Palli, B., & Kramer, L. *The aging worker and the union*. New York: Praeger, 1971.

Cottrell, F., & Atchley, R. *Women in retirement: A preliminary report*. Oxford, Ohio: Scripps Foundation, 1969.

Cox, D. *Analysis of binary data*. London: Chapman and Hall, 1970.

Daymont, T. Changes in black-white labor market opportunities, 1966-1976. In H. Parnes (Ed.), *Work and retirement: A longitudinal study of men*. Cambridge, Mass.: MIT Press, 1981.

Ekerdt, D., Bosse, R., & LoCastro, J. Claims that retirement improves health. *Journal of Gerontology*, 1983, *38*, 231-236.

Elwell, F., & Maltbie-Crannell, A. The impact of role loss upon coping resources and life satisfaction of the elderly. *Journal of Gerontology*, 1981, *36*, 223-232.

Epstein, L., & Murray, J. *The aged population of the U.S.* Washington, D.C.: U.S. Government Printing Office, 1967.

Fillenbaum, G.G. On the relation between attitude to work and attitude to retirement. *Journal of Gerontology*, 1971, *26*, 244-248. (a)

Fillenbaum, G.G. The working retired. *Journal of Gerontology*, 1971, *26*, 82-89. (b)

Fillenbaum, G.G., & Maddox, G.L. Work after retirement: An investigation into some psychologically relevant variables. *Gerontologist*, 1974, *14*, 418-424.

Fiske, M. Changing hierarchies of commitment in adulthood. In N.J. Smelser & E.H. Erikson (Eds.), *Themes of work and love in adulthood*. Cambridge, Mass.: Harvard University Press, 1980.

Fox, A. Work status and income change, 1968-72: Retirement History Study preview. *Social Security Bulletin*, 1976, *39* (12), 14-30.

Fox, A. Earnings replacement rates of retired couples: Findings from the Retirement History Study. *Social Security Bulletin*, 1979, *42* (1), 2-24.

Fox, J. Effects of retirement and former work life on women's adaptation in old age. *Journal of Gerontology*, 1977, *32*, 196-202.

Friedmann, E., & Havighurst, R. *The meaning of work and retirement*. Chicago, Ill.: University of Chicago Press, 1954.

Fujii, S. Minority group elderly: Demographic characteristics and implications for public policy. In C. Eisdorfer (Editor-in-chief), *Annual Review of Gerontology and Geriatrics* (Vol. 1). New York: Springer Publishing Co., 1980.

Gelfand, D., & Kutzik, A. (Eds.). *Ethnicity and aging: Theory, research and policy.* New York: Springer Publishing Co., 1979.

George, L. *Role transitions in later life.* Monterey, Ca.: Brooks/Cole, 1980.

George, L. Subjective well-being: Conceptual and methodological issues. In C. Eisdorfer (Ed.), *Annual Review of Gerontology and Geriatrics* (Vol. 2). New York: Springer Publishing Co., 1981.

George, L. Models of transitions in middle and later life. *Annals,* 1982, *464,* 22-38.

George, L. & Bearon, L. *Quality of life in older persons: meaning and measurement.* New York: Human Sciences Press, 1980.

George, L., & Landerman, L. Health and subjective well-being: A replicated secondary analysis. *International Journal of Aging and Human Development,* in press.

George, L., & Maddox, G. Subjective adaptation to loss of the work role: A longitudinal study. *Journal of Gerontology,* 1977, *32,* 356-362.

Glamser, F. The impact of preretirement programs on the retirement experience. *Journal of Gerontology,* 1981, *36,* 244-250.

Glamser, F., & DeJong, G. The efficacy of preretirement preparation programs for industrial workers. *Journal of Gerontology,* 1975, *30,* 595-600.

Gordon, R.H., & Blinder, A.S. Market wages, reservation wages and retirement decisions. *Journal of Public Economics,* 1980, *14,* 277-308.

Goudy, W.J., Powers, E.A., & Keith, P. The work-satisfaction, retirement-attitude typology: Profile examination. *Experimental Aging Research,* 1975, *1,* 267-279.

Graney, J.J., & Cottam, D.M. Labor force non-participation of older people: United States, 1890-1970. *The Gerontologist,* 1981, *21,* 138-141.

Gratton, B., & Haug, M. Decision and adaptation: Research on female retirement. *Journal of Gerontology,* 1983, *5,* 59-76.

Halperin, M., Blackwelder, W., & Verter, J. Estimation of the multivariate logistic risk function: A comparison of the discriminant function and maximum likelihood approaches. *Journal of Chronic Disease,* 1971, *24,* 125-158.

Hanushek, E., & Jackson, J. *Statistical methods for social scientists.* New York: Academic Press, 1977.

Harris, L. *Aging in the eighties.* Washington, D.C.: National Council on the Aging, 1981.

Havighurst, R., Neugarten, B., Munnichs, J., & Thomae, H. (Eds.). *Adjustment to retirement.* Netherlands: Van Gorkum, 1969.

Haynes, S., McMichael, A., & Tyroler, H. Survival after early and normal retirement. *Journal of Gerontology,* 1978, *33,* 269-279.

Herzog, A., Rodgers, W., & Woodworth, J. *Subjective well-being among different age groups.* Ann Arbor, Mich.: Institute for Social Research, 1982.

Hill, R. A demographic profile of the black elderly. *Aging,* 1978 (Sept.-Oct.), 2-9.

Hogan, D. The transition to adulthood as a career contingency. *American Sociological Review,* 1980, *45,* 261-276.

Irelan, L. Retirement history study: Introduction. *Social Security Bulletin,* 1972, *35* (11), 3-8.

Jaslow, P. Employment, retirement, and morale among older women. *Journal of Gerontology,* 1976, *31,* 212-218.

Jencks, C. Discrimination and Thomas Sowell. Part I. *New York Review of Books,* 1983, *30* (3), 33-38.

Jessor, R., Groves, T., Hansen, R., & Jessor, S. *Society, personality and deviant behavior.* New York: Holt, Reinhart, and Winston, 1968.

Keith, P. Working women versus homemakers: Retirement resources and correlates of well-being. In M. Szinovacz (Ed.), *Women's retirement.* Beverly Hills, Ca.: Sage Publications, 1982.

Kell, D., & Patton, C.V. Reaction to induced early retirement. *The Gerontologist,* 1978, *18,* 173-179.

Kelleher, C.H., & Quirk, D.A. Age, functional capacity and work: An annotated bibliography. *Industrial Gerontology,* 1973, *19,* 80-98.

Kimmel, D., Price, K., & Walker, J. Retirement choice and retirement satisfaction. *Journal of Gerontology,* 1978, *33,* 575-585.

Kroeger, N. Preretirement preparation: Sex differences in access, sources, and use. In M. Szinovacz (Ed.), *Women's retirement.* Beverly Hills, Ca.: Sage Publications, 1982.

Larson, R. Thirty years of research on the subjective well-being of older Americans. *Journal of Gerontology,* 1978, *33,* 109-129.

Liang, J., & Warfel, B. Urbanism and life satisfaction among the aged. *Journal of Gerontology,* 1983, *38,* 97-106.

Marini, M. The transition to adulthood: Sex differences in educational attainment and age at marriage. *American Sociological Review,* 1978, *43,* 483-507.

McClosky, H., & Schaar, J. Psychological dimensions of anomy. *American Sociological Review,* 1965, *30,* 14-40.

MacMillan, A. The Health Opinion Survey: Technique for estimating prevalence of psychoneurotic and related types of disorder in communities. *Psychological Reports,* 1957, *3,* 325-339.

Miller, S. The social dilemma of the aging leisure participant. In A. Rose & W. Peterson (Eds.), *Older people and their social world.* Philadelphia: Davis, 1965.

Minkler, M. Research on the health effects of retirement. *Journal of Health and Social Behavior,* 1981, *22,* 117-130.

Morgan, J. Retirement in prospect and retrospect. In J. Morgan & G. Duncan (Eds.), *Five thousand American families* (Vol. VIII). Ann Arbor, Mich.: Institute for Social Research, 1980.

Morgan, J. Antecedents and consequences of retirement. In M. Hill, O. Hill, & J. Morgan (Eds.), *Five thousand American families* (Vol. IX). Ann Arbor, Mich.: Institute for Social Research, 1981.

Morgan, J., & Duncan, G. (Eds.), *Five thousand American families* (Vol. VIII). Ann Arbor, Mich.: Institute for Social Research, 1980.

Motley, D. Availability of retired persons for work. *Social Security Bulletin*, 1978, *41*(4), 18-28.

Murray, J. Subjective retirement. *Social Security Bulletin*, 1979, *42*, 1-7.

Mutran, E., & Reitzes, D. Retirement, identity and well-being: Realignment of role relationships. *Journal of Gerontology*, 1981, *36*, 733-740.

Nadelson, T. A survey of the literature on the adjustment of the aged to retirement. *Journal of Geriatric Psychiatry*, 1969, *3*, 3-20.

Newman, E., Sherman, S., & Higgins, C. Retirement expectations and plans: A comparison of men and women. In M. Szinovacz (Ed.), *Women's retirement.* Beverly Hills, Ca.: Sage Publications, 1982.

Okun, M., Stock, W., Haring, M., & Witter, R. Health and subjective well-being: A meta-analysis. *International Journal of Aging and Human Development,* in press.

O'Rand, A., & Henretta, J. Midlife work history and retirement income. In M. Szinovacz (Ed.), *Women's retirement.* Beverly Hills, Ca.: Sage Publications, 1982.

Palmore, E. Employment and retirement. In Epstein, L. (Ed.), *The aged population of the United States.* Washington, D.C.: U.S. Government Printing Office, 1967.

Palmore, E. (Ed.). *Normal aging I.* Durham, N.C.: Duke University Press, 1970.

Palmore, E. Why do people retire? *Aging and Human Development.* 1971, *2*, 269-283.

Palmore, E. (Ed.). *Normal aging II.* Durham, N.C.: Duke University Press, 1974.

Palmore, E. When can age, period, and cohort be separated? *Social Forces*, 1978, *57*, 282-295.

Palmore, E. *Social patterns in normal aging.* Durham, N.C.: Duke University Press, 1981.

Palmore, E., Fillenbaum, G., & George, L. Consequences of retirement. *Journal of Gerontology*, 1984, *39*, 109-116.

Palmore, E., George, L., & Fillenbaum, G. Predictors of retirement. *Journal of Gerontology*, 1982, *37*, 733-742.

Parnes, H. *Work and retirement.* Cambridge, Mass.: Massachusetts Institute of Technology Press, 1981.

Parnes, H., & Nestel, G. *Retirement expectations of middle-aged men.* Columbus, Ohio: Center for Human Resources Research, Ohio State University, 1971.

Parnes, H., & Nestel, G. The retirement experience. In H.S. Parnes (Ed.), *Work and retirement: A longitudinal study of men.* Cambridge, Mass.: MIT Press, 1981.

Peretti, P., & Wilson, C. Voluntary and involuntary retirement of aged males and their effect on emotional satisfaction, usefulness, self-image, emotional stability, and interpersonal relationships. *International Journal of Aging and Human Development,* 1975, *6,* 131-138.

Press, S., & Wilson, S. Choosing between logistic regression and discriminant analysis. *Journal of American Statistical Association,* 1978, *73,* 699-705.

Program Analysis Staff. Mortality and early retirement. *Social Security Bulletin,* 1982, *45,* 3-10.

Quinn, J.F. The extent and correlates of partial retirement. *The Gerontologist,* 1981, *21,* 634-643.

Rhine, S. *Older workers and retirement.* New York: The Conference Board, Inc., 1978.

Rodgers, G. Vesting of private pension benefits in 1979 and change from 1972. *Social Security Bulletin,* 1981, *44* (7), 12-27.

Rosow, I. One moral dilemma of an affluent society. *The Gerontologist,* 1962, *2,* 189-191.

Schiller, B.R., & Snyder, D.C. Restrictive pension provisions and the older worker. *The Gerontologist,* 1982, *22,* 482-487.

Schmidt, P., & Sickles, R. Some further evidence on the use of the Chow test under heteroskedasticity. *Econometrica,* 1977, *45,* 1293-1298.

Schulz, J. et al. *Providing adequate retirement income.* Hanover, N.H.: University Press of New England, 1974. (2nd ed., 1980.)

Schwab, K. Early labor force withdrawal of men: participants and nonparticipants aged 58-63. In L. M. Irelan, D. K. Motley, K. Schwab, S. R. Sherman, & J. Murray (Eds.), *Almost 65: Baseline data from the Retirement History Study.* Research Report No. 49, Social Security Administration, HEW Publications No. (SSA) 76-11806, 1976.

Schwab, K. Early labor-force withdrawal of men. In L. Irelan (Ed.), *Almost 65,* Washington, D.C.: U.S. Government Printing Office, 1976.

Shanas, E., Townsend, P., Wedderbum, D., Friis, H., Milhoj, P., & Stehouwer, J. *Older people in three industrial societies.* New York: Atherton Press, 1968.

Shanas, E. Adjustment to retirement. In F. Carp (Ed.), *Retirement.* New York: Behavioral Publications, 1972.

Sheppard, H. Work and retirement. In R. H. Binstock & E. Shanas (Eds.), *Handbook of aging and the social sciences.* New York: Van Nostrand Reinhold, 1976.

Simpson, I., & McKinney, J. (Eds.). *Social aspects of aging.* Durham, N.C.: Duke University Press, 1966.

Simpson, I., Back, K., & McKinney, J. Attributes of work, involvement in society, and self-evaluation in retirement. In I. H. Simpson & J. C. McKinney (Eds.), *Social aspects of aging.* Durham, N.C.: Duke University Press, 1966. (a)

Simpson, I., Back, K., & McKinney, J. Orientations toward work and retirement and self-evaluation in retirement. In I. Simpson & J. McKinney

(Eds.), *Social aspects of aging.* Durham, N.C.: Duke University Press, 1966. (b)

Simpson, I., Back, K., & McKinney, J. Exposure to information on, preparation for, and self-evaluation in retirement. In I. H. Simpson & J. C. McKinney (Eds.), *Social aspects of aging.* Durham, N.C.: Duke University Press, 1966. (c)

Simpson, I., Back, K., & McKinney, J. Continuity of work and retirement activities and self-evaluation. In I. H. Simpson & J. C. McKinney (Eds.), *Social aspects of aging.* Durham, N.C.: Duke University Press, 1966. (d)

Social Security Bulletin. Low income aged: Eligibility and participation in SSI. 1982, *45* (5), 28-35.

Soumerai, S. B, & Avorn, J. Perceived health, life satisfaction, and activity in urban elderly: A controlled study of the impact of part-time work. *Journal of Gerontology*, 1983, *38*, 356-362.

Sowell, T. *Ethnic America.* New York: Basic Books, 1981.

Stagner, R. Propensity to work: An important variable in retiree behavior. *Aging and Work*, 1979, *2*, 161-172.

Stokes, R., & Maddox, G. Some social factors in retirement adaptation. *Journal of Gerontology*, 1968, *22*, 329-333.

Streib, G. F, & Schneider, C. J. *Retirement in American society: Impact and process.* Ithaca, N.Y.: Cornell University Press, 1971.

Szinovacz, M. (Ed.). *Women's retirement: Policy implications of recent research* (Vol. 6). Sage Yearbooks in Women's Studies, Beverly Hills, Ca.: Sage Publications, 1982.

Tatsuoka, M. *Multivariate analysis: Techniques for educational and psychological research.* New York: Wiley, 1971.

Thompson, G. Work versus leisure roles. *Journal of Gerontology*, 1973, *28*, 339-344.

Thompson, G. Work experience and income of the population aged 60 and older. *Social Security Bulletin*, 1974, *37*, 3-20.

Thompson, G. Black-white differences in private pensions: Findings from the Retirement History Study. *Social Security Bulletin*, 1979, *42* (2), 15-22.

Thompson, W. Pre-retirement anticipation and adjustment in retirement. *Journal of Social Issues*, 1958, *14*, 35-45.

Thompson, W., & Streib, G. Situational determinants, health and economic deprivation in retirement. *Journal of Social Issues*, 1958, *14*, 18-34.

Townsend, P. *Poverty in the United Kingdom: A survey of household resources and standards of living.* Harmondsworth, Middlesex, England: Penguin Books, Ltd., 1979.

U.S. Department of Commerce, Bureau of the Census. *Statistical Abstract of the United States, 1976* (97th ed.), Washington, D.C., 1976.

Walker, G., & Duncan, D. Estimation of the probability of an event as a function of several independent variables. *Biometrika*, 1967, *54*, 167-179.

Wentworth, E. C. *Employment after retirement.* Research Report No. 21.
    Office of Research and Statistics, Social Security Administration,
    U.S. Department of Health, Education and Welfare, Washington,
    D.C., 1968.
Wilensky, H. Work careers, and social integration. *International Social Science
    Journal,* 1960, *12*, 543-560.

Appendix
Variables

The following are the definitions and codes of all variables used in the tables. Only statistically significant variables are included in the tables. The variables are arranged in alphabetical order within study, and the studies are arranged alphabetically.

Duke Second Longitudinal Survey Variables

Age: age in years

Age Identification: subjective age group identification, with not old = 0; old = 1.

Anomie: summed scores of 6 variables, each of which is dichotomous. Scores range from 0 to 12, with higher scores indicating greater level of anomie.

Church Attendance: number of times a month respondent attends religious services.

Education: highest grade attended, measured in years.

Future Orientation: coded from 1 to 7, with higher scores indicating greater future (as opposed to past) orientation.

Health: respondent's subjective assessment of his health, with 1 = poor; 2 = fair; 3 = good; 4 = excellent.

Income: total income from all sources, with 0 = under $1000; 1 = $1000-$1,999; 2 = $2000-$2,999; 3 = $3,000-$3,999; 4 = $4,000-$4,999; 5 = $5,000-$5,999; 6 = $6,000-$6,999; 7 = $7,000-$9,999; 8 = $10,000-$14,999; 9 = $15,000 and over.

Internal Orientation: locus of control, summed scores on 11 variables. Higher scores indicate greater internal orientation.

Life Satisfaction: Cantril Ladder measure. Scores ranged from 0 to 9, with higher scores indicating higher life satisfaction.

Negative Affect: summed scores on questions measuring perceived boredom, depression, loneliness, and restlessness.

Coded from 0 to 12, with higher scores indicating greater negative feelings.

Non-employment work: number of hours spent weekly on yard care, gardening, repairing, building, mending, sewing, and other such activities.

Objective Retirement: working less than full-time (no pension data).

Psychosomatic Symptoms: the sum of scores on nine variables, which measure the frequency of dizziness, general aches and pains, headaches, muscle twitches or trembling, nervousness or tenseness, rapid heart beat, sleeplessness, loss of appetite, constipation. The variable is measured from 0 to 27, with higher scores indicating greater symptoms.

Reason for Retirement: indicates whether retirement was due to health, compulsory reasons or voluntary.

Self-care Activity: number of hours spent weekly eating, dressing, bathing, and personal care.

Sex: male = 1; female = 2.

Social Value: the sum of scores on variables measuring effectiveness, satisfaction with life, and feelings of respect, coded from 3 to 21, with higher scores indicating greater social value.

Solitary Activity: number of hours spent weekly watching TV, reading newspapers, magazines, or books, playing a sport or working on a hobby, and watching sports events.

Time Spent with Friends: number of hours spent weekly visiting, telephoning, or writing friends or relatives, at parties, eating out, or entertaining.

Usefulness: sum of scores measuring perceived usefulness, level of activity, and extent to which respondent is free to do things. Coded from 3 to 21, with higher scores indicating greater usefulness.

Duke Work and Retirement Study Variables

Friends Seen: actual number of friends seen per week.

Health Compared with Others: Scored from 1 to 9, with higher scores indicating better health.

Sense of Autonomy: semantic differential score. Coded from 4 to 28, with higher scores indicating greater sense of autonomy.

National Longitudinal Survey Variables

Age: age at last birthday.

Age at Retirement: age at the wave in which the respondent first met the criteria for objective retirement.

Annual Hours Worked: number of hours employed in the past year.

Area Unemployment: unemployment rate in local area coded from 1 for low to 5 for high unemployment.

Assets: respondent's net family assets, excluding automobiles, 1976.

Core Industry: agricultural, sales, service, & professional industries = 0; construction and production industries = 1.

Early Retirement: retired prior to age 65 according to objective retirement definition.

Education: number of years of education completed.

Employed by Others: self-employed = 0; employed by others = 1.

Food Stamps: respondent did not receive government food stamps in 1975 = 0; respondent did receive food stamps = 1.

Health Factor: respondent's overall health rating. Based on questions concerning his attitude toward his health condition, whether he has experienced health problems, and his health condition over the past three years. Coded from 0 to 8, with higher scores indicating better health ratings.

Health Limits: health does not limit work = 0; health limits work = 1.

Health Rating: respondent's comparison of own health to that of other men: poor = 1; fair = 2; good = 3; excellent = 4.

Health Satisfaction: respondent's attitude toward his health condition, with very unhappy = 1; somewhat unhappy = 2; somewhat happy = 3; and very happy = 4.

Income: 1975 family income, measured in dollars.

Internal Orientation: based on Rotter "Locus of Control" scale which has 11 pairs of statements from which respondent picks one as "more true than the other." High scores indicate high internal orientation.

Job Attitude: dislikes current job very much = 1; dislikes somewhat = 2; likes fairly well = 3; likes very much = 4.

Job Hours per Year: usual number of hours respondent works per year.

Leisure Satisfaction: respondent's attitude toward leisure time activities, with very unhappy = 1, somewhat unhappy = 2, somewhat happy = 3; and very happy = 4.

Life Satisfaction: respondent's attitude toward life overall, with very unhappy = 1, somewhat unhappy = 2, somewhat happy = 3, and very happy = 4.

Living Standard: respondent's attitude toward standard of living, with very unhappy = 1; somewhat unhappy = 2; somewhat happy = 3; very happy = 4.

Mandatory Retirement: no mandatory retirement age at job = 0; job has mandatory retirement age = 1.

Number Children under 18: number of children under 18 in household.

Number of Employers: number of employers worked for in 1965.

Objective Retirement: working less than 35 hours per week (pension data was incomplete).

Occupation: first digit code of the Census Bureau's Occupational Index Code, recoded so that higher values indicate higher status.

Pension: job not covered by pension plan = 0; job covered by pension plan = 1.

Poverty Ratio: ratio of respondent's family income to 1965 poverty level.

Race: white = 1; nonwhite = 2.

Reason for Retirement: three dummy variables, indicating whether respondent retired because of health reasons, because it was compulsory, or whether he retired voluntarily.

Retirement Attitude: respondent's propensity for retirement with higher scores indicating greater propensity. Based on responses to questions asking if respondent would work if he did not have to, would retire if he lost his job, whether he expects to retire at a compulsory retirement age, expected age of retirement, reasons for expected age of retirement, and whether he expects to work after retirement.

Residence Satisfaction: respondent's attitude toward his area of residence, with very unhappy = 1, somewhat unhappy =2, somewhat happy = 3, and very happy = 4.

Self-employed: employed = 0; self-employed = 1.

SSI: respondent does not receive income from Supplemental Security Income (SSI) checks = 0; respondent does receive SSI checks = 1.

Wage: annual salary or wages in $1000 intervals.

Work Limitations: no health-related work limitations = 0; health-related work limitations = 1.

Work More Important Than Wages: wages are more important than liking work = 1; liking work is more important than wages = 2.

Ohio Longitudinal Survey Variables

Health: respondent's self-rating of his health, with very poor = 1; poor = 2; fair = 3; good = 4; very good = 5.

Social Withdrawal: scale, scored 1 to 20, with higher scores indicating less withdrawal.

Panel Study of Income Dynamics Variables

Health Limits: whether or not the respondent has health limits on the amount or type of work he can do, with no limits = 0 and work is limited = 1.

Income: total family income in 1967, measured in dollars.

Income Adequacy: 1967 family income divided by poverty level income.

Poverty Ratio: respondent's decile score of income adequacy.

Retirement History Survey Variables

Activity Satisfaction: factor based on the frequency with which respondent met his neighbors, phoned neighbors and friends, and attended religious services.

Age: age at last birthday.

Annual Hours Worked: number of hours employed during past two years, in thousands.

Early Retirement: retired prior to age 65 according to objective retirement definition.

Education: number of years of education completed.

Extra-Work Interests: factor based on the number of dependents, the frequency with which hobbies are pursued, and the frequency of home maintenance.

Formal Organizations: factor based on the number of organizations contributed to, the number of professional organizations in which the respondent is a member, number of magazines and newspapers subscribed to, frequency of attending clubs, and the frequency of doing volunteer work.

Health Factor: factorially derived measure of respondent's health, based on information on presence of any health limitation, whether health limits work, the duration of health limitation, and respondent's health compared to that of others. Higher scores indicated poorer health.

Health Limits: no health limitations on mobility = 0; health limitations on mobility = 1.

Health Rating: respondent's rating of his own health compared to others, with worse = 1; same = 2; better = 3.

Income: annual income from all sources, measured in dollars.

Income Adequacy: a scale based on the ratio of family income to the Federal Intermediate Budget level adjusted for the number of dependents. The scale ranges from 6 (excellent) for those with a ratio of 2 or more, to 1 (poor) for those with a ratio of less than .37.

Index